Dr. Carol E. Hoffecker

DELAWARE,
The First State

Dr. Carol E. Hoffecker

DELAWARE, The First State

A Delaware Heritage Commission book commemorating the 200th anniversary of the United States Constitution and Delaware's ratification as ''The First State.''

Publication made possible through a grant from The National Society of The Colonial Dames of America in the State of Delaware

THE MIDDLE ATLANTIC PRESS
Wilmington, Delaware

DELAWARE, THE FIRST STATE

A MIDDLE ATLANTIC PRESS BOOK

A Delaware Heritage Commission book,
commemorating the ratification of the
United States Constitution by Delaware, "The First State"

First Middle Atlantic Press printing, February 1988

ISBN: 0-912608-47-1

The Middle Atlantic Press, Inc.
848 Church Street
Wilmington, Delaware

Library of Congress Cataloging-in-Publication Data
Hoffecker, Carol E.
    Delaware, the first state.

    Summary: Examines the history of Delaware, from its first inhabitants and the arrival of European settlers to the effect of modern times on its business and government.
    1. Delaware—History—Juvenile literature.
[1. Delaware—History]   I. Delaware Heritage Commission.
II. Title.
F164.3.H64   1987   975.1   87-11200
ISBN 0-912608-47-1

Manufactured in the United States of America

Table of Contents

Delaware's Heritage

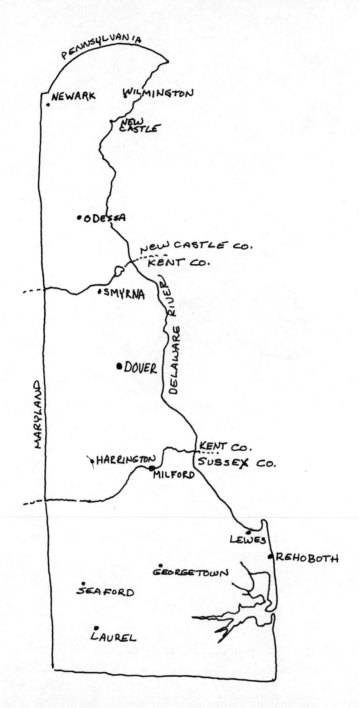

Map of Delaware showing county lines and major towns

UNIT ONE

DISCOVERING DELAWARE

CHAPTER ONE

What Is Delaware?

WELCOME TO DELAWARE. Delaware is one of the fifty states that make up the United States of America. The rules that unite the United States are called the *Constitution.* Delaware was the first state to agree to the United States Constitution when our country was just getting started. That is why Delawareans are proud to call their state the First State.

In this book you will learn many things about Delaware, about its history, its people, its communities, its natural resources, and its economy. The things that you learn will help you to understand why and how Delaware got to be the way it is today. You will also learn about Delaware's role in the United States and about the goals that Delawareans like you may have for the future.

Let us start by looking at a map of the United States of America. Can you find Delaware on the map? Delaware is hard to find because it is a very small state. In fact, it is the second smallest state in the nation. Only Rhode Island is smaller. You will notice that Delaware's nearest neighbors are the states of Maryland, Pennsylvania, and New Jersey.

Delaware is surrounded by water on three sides. The Delaware River, Delaware Bay, and the Atlantic Ocean are to the east of Delaware. Delaware's western border

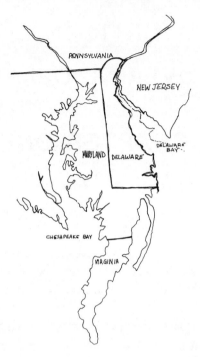

Map of Delmarva Peninsula and surroundings

connects the First State to a part of Maryland that is called the *eastern* shore because it is *east* of the Chesapeake Bay. Delaware, the eastern shore of Maryland, and a little piece of Virginia form a *peninsula* called the Delmarva Peninsula. A peninsula is a strip of land that has water on three sides. Why do you think this peninsula was given the name Delmarva? Can you find another peninsula on the map of the United States? Which state is it in?

Water has played a very important role in Delaware's history, and it continues to be an important resource today. Delaware has an area of 2,057 square miles. Seventy-five of those square miles consist of water in the Delaware River and Delaware Bay. Nearly 190 square miles of Delaware's land consists of tidal wetlands. The wetlands are low marsh lands along Delaware's coast next to the Delaware Bay and the Delaware River. The

Delaware's tidal wetlands
Courtesy of Hagley Museum and Library

wetlands are the meeting ground of the land and the sea. The ocean tides bring salt water into them that mixes with the fresh water from inland streams. The wetlands provide a good environment for many fish, birds, and other animals. We will learn more about the importance of Delaware's coastal wetlands later in this book.

Most of Delaware is flat. That is because nearly all of Delaware is part of the *Atlantic coastal plain*. Thousands of years ago, when ice at the North and South poles melted and the oceans became bigger, the coastal plain was covered by water. Then the oceans became smaller, leaving flat land not far above sea level, known as the coastal plain. The lowland of the coastal plain is sandy and does not contain large rocks. The rivers and streams of the plain are shallow and move slowly in snakelike patterns across the flat land.

Only one small part of Delaware is not in the coastal plain. The northwest corner of the state is part of the *Piedmont Plateau*. Imagine a line drawn between Newark and Wilmington. The Piedmont Plateau lies northwest of that line. The Piedmont Plateau runs from north to south through the eastern United States between the

The Brandywine Valley, part of the Piedmont Plateau
Courtesy of Hagley Museum and Library

Appalachian Mountains and the coastal plain. The word "piedmont" means "foothill," so the Piedmont Plateau is at the foot of the mountains that lie west of Delaware in central Pennsylvania.

Land in the Piedmont Plateau is hilly and high above sea level. The highest point in Delaware is 442 feet above sea level. The soil of the Piedmont Plateau is filled with stones and rocks. The streams and rivers of the plateau move swiftly down the hills to the coastal plain below. The point where these rivers reach the flat plain is called the *fall line*. The fall line marks the division between the plateau and the plain. Cities and towns are often located at the fall lines of the larger rivers because ships cannot sail uphill into the plateau. Therefore, the fall line is the place where overland transportation and water transportation meet.

Delaware has a mild climate. The average temperature in January, the coldest month, is 34°F., just above freezing. The average temperature in July, the hottest month, is about 75° F. The highest temperature ever recorded in Delaware was 105° F. and the lowest was −12° F. Because of this mild weather Delaware's farmers have a long growing season and ice storms do not do

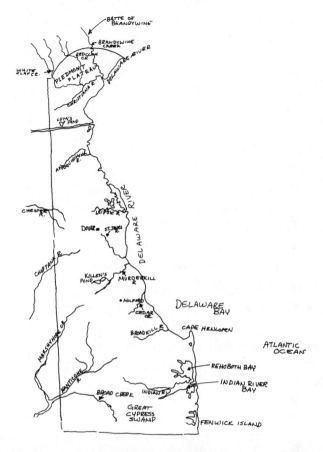

Topographical map of Delaware showing plateau and plain

much damage. Delaware receives about 45 inches of rain and snow each year. Good rainfall is important to the farmers.

Sometimes Delaware experiences heavy storms that can do a great deal of damage. Northeasters are heavy rainstorms that bring great gusts of wind and make large ocean waves. These storms come from the northeast. That is why they are called "Northeasters." One Northeaster, in March 1962, destroyed the boardwalk and many homes and hotels at Rehoboth Beach. The storm whipped up the ocean and big waves attacked the beach, destroying everything in their path.

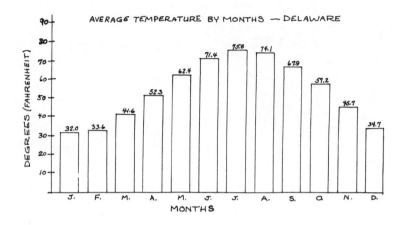

Chart showing Delaware's average temperature by month

Sometimes hurricanes come to Delaware. Hurricanes start in the Caribbean Sea during the fall and move north. Like Northeasters, they bring heavy rains, high seas, and powerful winds that can topple big trees. Fortunately, these storms do not strike Delaware very often.

Destruction by "Northeaster" at Rehoboth Beach, 1962
Courtesy of Delaware State Archives

CHAPTER TWO

Delaware's First People

FOUR HUNDRED YEARS ago, marshes, forests, and meadows covered all of the land that we call Delaware. Many animals lived on the land. Families of beavers built log dams across small streams. Large herds of whitetailed deer ate the leaves of forest trees and bushes. Wolves hunted other animals. Many turtles, oysters, fish, and crabs lived in Delaware's coastal streams and marshes. The cries of wild geese and turkeys filled the autumn air. Hawks, eagles, and many other types of birds made their homes here also.

The people who lived in Delaware in those days were the *Lenni Lenape* Indians. The name Lenni Lenape means "common people" in the Indian language. The Lenni Lenape were a peace-loving tribe. They lived in the area from where New York City is today, in the north, down through New Jersey, southeastern Pennsylvania, and

Indian man, hunting.

7

most of Delaware. The European settlers called the Lenni Lenape the Delaware Indians because they lived on both sides of the Delaware River. Descendants of the Delaware Indians are still living today, but they have moved west and now live in the state of Oklahoma. A tribe related to the Lenni Lenape, called the *Nanticoke* Indians, lived in southwestern Delaware. Some Nanticoke Indians still live in Delaware today.

Even though the Lenni Lenape once lived in the same places that we live in today, their lives were very different from ours. The Lenni Lenape lived in villages located along the banks of streams and rivers where they

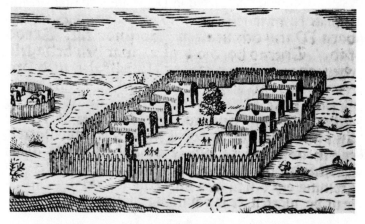

A Lenni Lenape village, as imagined by a 17th-century artist
Courtesy of The Historical Society of Delaware

could find food and water. Each Indian family lived in a small house made of bark. They called their houses *wigwams*. The Indians slept in their wigwams, but they spent most of their time outdoors.

The Lenni Lenape were skilled hunters, fishermen, and farmers. They made their houses, tools, and clothing from the things that they found around them. They made canoes by hollowing out logs. They made pots for storing and cooking food from clay. They made clothing from the skins of animals and the feathers of birds. They made bows from tree branches and the sinews or ten-

Lenni Lenape artifacts
Courtesy of Hagley Museum and Library

dons of animals. Arrows came from feathers, straight sticks, and stones sharpened to a point.

Indian parents did different jobs in order to support their families. The men cleared land, built wigwams, and protected the family from danger. Using bows and arrows, the men hunted animals for food and clothing. They also fished and collected clams, oysters, and crabs. The Indians fished by building a stone dam called a *weir* across a shallow river. The dam had a narrow opening in the center. When the fish swam to the opening the Indian men would spear them or catch them in nets.

The Lenni Lenape women took care of the babies and small children. They also made clothing and baskets, kept the fires going, and cooked the food. Women grew the crops. Farming was very important to the Indians because it provided corn. Corn was the food they ate most often. In addition to corn, the women grew beans, pumpkins, squash, and tobacco.

An Indian mother prepared a variety of meals from the foods she grew. Sometimes she roasted corn on the cob. Other times she cut the kernels off the cob and cooked them with beans to make succotash. The Indian mother also dried corn kernels in the sun and then pounded and ground them into cornmeal. From cornmeal, Indian women made bread and mush, which is like a hot cereal. Indian children particularly liked to eat corn meal mixed with maple sugar.

Mothers kept their babies close by them as they farmed and did their other chores. They strapped the baby to a flat cradle board so that they could carry the baby on their backs or hang the cradle from a tree. The parents taught their children about the trees, plants, animals, fish, and birds. Fathers taught their sons to fish and hunt. Mothers taught their daughters to plant crops, tan hides, sew clothing, and cook food. By the time the children were six or seven years old, they were able to

Indian woman at work grinding corn.

help their parents with many chores. The children's help was very important to the family.

The Lenni Lenape liked to dress up by wearing colorful jewelry. They made beads from sea shells and stones. They traded with other tribes to get different colored stones from far away. They painted their bodies with paints made from berries and other plants. Both men and women tattooed their bodies. They made tattoos by puncturing their skin with a sharp stone or bone and putting powdered tree bark into the skin. The tattoos pictured snakes, birds, or other animals.

A young man shaved the hair from most of his head but left a small clump shaped like a cock's comb in the center. He put bear grease onto the cock's comb to make it stand up straight. He attached an eagle feather to his hair to give him the courage of the eagle. In the summer the Indians wore little clothing. They covered their bodies with bear grease to keep mosquitos and other insects from biting them.

Every Lenni Lenape village had a chief who was the leader. The chief ruled with a council made up of the older men of the village. When a chief was about to die, he selected a new chief. Although the chief was more powerful than other people in the village, he did not have a bigger wigwam or more possessions. The Indians did not think it was useful to own more than they needed to survive. Nature itself gave pleasure to the Lenni Lenape, and nature was open to everybody.

All Lenni Lenape loved and respected nature. They learned this respect from their parents. Their way of life and their religion depended on this lesson. The Lenni Lenape never wasted anything. They did not kill more fish, birds, or animals than they needed to eat or to make clothing. They did not chop down a tree unless

Indian elder telling creation story.

they needed the land for crops or needed the tree to make a canoe or a building. Because they were careful not to destroy nature, they had plenty of food to eat.

The Lenni Lenape believed the Great Spirit controlled the earth, the sun, the moon, and the stars. The Great Spirit had created lesser spirits that controlled the winds, rivers, trees, and animals. Some animals were particularly important because of the spirits that lived in them. These special animals were the wolf, the wild turkey, and the turtle.

When the Europeans first came to America, they asked the Lenni Lenape about their religion. One question they asked was "How did the world begin?" An old Indian answered that question. He sat silently for a few minutes. Then he took a piece of coal from the edge of the fire and drew a picture on the floor. The picture showed a turtle. The Indian told the white man that long ago the world had been nothing but water. A giant turtle lived under the water. The turtle raised its back out of the water and its back became the land. When the land dried, a tree grew in the middle of the giant turtle's

Archaeologists at work
Courtesy of State of Delaware, Department of Natural Resources, Division of
Parks and Recreation

back. One of the tree's roots became the first man. The man was lonely so the tree bent over until its top touched the ground. When the tree straightened up, a new root sprang up that became the first woman.

We do not know exactly how long the Lenni Lenape lived in Delaware. Scientists who study remains of human settlements that are buried in the ground are called *archaeologists*. In Delaware, the archaeologists have learned that Indians lived along the coast of the Delaware Bay many centuries before the Europeans came to America. The archaeologists' most important discovery in Delaware so far is the Island Field Site near Delaware Bay. By digging at the Island Field, the archaeologists have learned many things about how the Indians lived.

CHAPTER THREE
European Discovery

IN THE YEAR 1492, a very brave sea captain set out on a voyage of discovery that changed the world. The sea captain's name was Christopher Columbus. He wanted to find the shortest route to China. Since he knew that the earth was round, he believed that if he sailed west from Europe he would come to China. King Ferdinand and Queen Isabella of Spain believed that Columbus was right. They gave him three ships called the *Nina*, the *Pinta*, and the *Santa Maria*, and he set sail westward from Spain.

Columbus's voyage did not turn out as he had planned. He did not find China. Instead he found the continent of America. He called the people he met "Indians" because he thought they lived in the "Indies" of Asia. He did not know that he had found the New World. On a globe, find Spain and China. Now find America. You can see why Columbus discovered America while sailing to China.

In the years after 1492 Columbus made several other trips to America. The Spanish sent other explorers to America as well. Some of the explorers discovered gold and silver in South America. The Spanish king and queen wanted these riches. They declared that all of America discovered by their explorers belonged to Spain. This land included the Caribbean Islands, Mexico, and most of the continent of South America.

When the other European countries learned about Spain's good fortune they started sending explorers to America too. John Cabot and his son Sebastian Cabot discovered Newfoundland in 1497, while exploring for England. Newfoundland is now part of Canada. Because

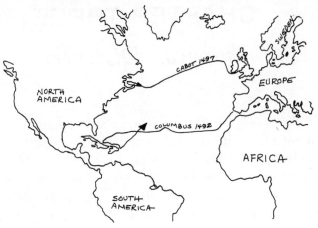

Map showing Western Europe and America and major voyages of exploration

of the Cabots' voyage, England claimed the coast of North America. France and Holland also sent explorers to North America. Holland, which is also called "the Netherlands," is a small flat country in northwestern Europe. Find the Netherlands on a map and you will see that it looks out to the ocean. The people who live in the Netherlands are called the Dutch. Four hundred years ago, the Netherlands was just as small as it is today, but it was a very important country because it had many merchants and trading ships. The Dutch established colonies around the world as bases for their trade.

In 1609 the Dutch hired an English explorer named Henry Hudson to find a shorter passage to Asia. Henry Hudson and his crew sailed to America on a ship called the *Half Moon*. Hudson hoped he could find a river that would lead from the Atlantic Ocean to the Pacific Ocean. He found several large bodies of water along America's Atlantic coast. He discovered the Delaware Bay and the Hudson River. He was disappointed to find that neither of them led to the Pacific Ocean. But he had made very important new discoveries.

Imagine how surprised the Lenni Lenape Indians must have been when they looked out on their familiar bay

Henry Hudson's *Half Moon*
Courtesy of The Historical Society of Delaware

and saw the *Half Moon*! Do you think they were curious about the big ship with its tall masts and white sails? Or do you think they were afraid? The *Half Moon* did not stay in the Delaware Bay very long. Henry Hudson could see that the bay was wide but that many parts of it were not very deep. He feared that his ship might get stuck on one of the many underwater sand bars called *shoals*.

A year or so later, other Dutch ships began coming to the Delaware Bay to trade with the Indians. They were careful to *take soundings* by putting a long rope attached to a metal cylinder over the side of the ship into the water to determine how deep the water was. In this way they did not get stuck on shoals. The Dutch sailors were amazed by the beauty of the new land and by the great number of fish, birds, and animals that they saw. They noticed the marshes that were rich with marine life and the big clumps of pine trees near the entrance to the bay. They could smell the sweet aroma of the trees before they sighted the land.

The Dutch traders found that the Lenni Lenape did not have gold or silver to sell and that their colorful jewels were not made from precious stones. The Dutchmen did not want to buy corn to take back to Holland because the Dutch could grow or buy food at home. There was, however, one thing that the Lenni Lenape had that the Dutch wanted to buy. That was furs. The Dutch could sell furs in Europe to make coats and hats. The beavers who built dams across the streams in the new land had very warm, pretty fur. They were also easy to catch. The Dutch traders told the Lenni Lenape that they would give them useful objects in return for the beaver furs.

But what could the Dutch sell to the Indians? Remember what we learned about the way the Indians lived? Remember what kinds of tools the Indians used and what kind of clothing they wore? When you read about the Indians did you notice that they did not have woven cloth or metal tools or guns? The Lenni Lenape were amazed by the wonderful things that the Dutchmen gave them for beaver skins. They liked to wear woven wool blankets. They liked to cook in iron pots. They liked to shoot guns. But the Indians did not know how to make these objects. The only way they could get them was to kill the beaver, foxes, bears, and other furry animals and then trade their skins for blankets, pots, and guns.

The Dutch built several trading posts in America. Their most important trading post was on the tip of Manhattan Island, where the Hudson River meets the Atlantic Ocean. They built this trading post in 1624 and called it New Amsterdam. It was named for Amsterdam, which was the largest city in Holland. New Amsterdam became the capital of the Dutch colonies in America. Today it is New York City. Can you find this city on a map?

In addition to furs, the Dutch wanted another product from the Delaware Bay. They wanted whale oil to burn

Model of Zwaanendael fort
Courtesy of State of Delaware, Division of Historical and Cultural Affairs

in lamps. The Dutchmen who came to the bay and river noticed many whales in the bay. In 1631 a group of Dutchmen organized a colony to capture the whales. They named the colony *Zwaanendael,* which means "Valley of the Swans," because they saw many swans there.

Zwaanendael was located just inside Cape Henlopen. A *cape* is a point of land that juts out into the water. Cape Henlopen separates the Atlantic Ocean from the Delaware Bay. Zwaanendael was just inside of Cape Henlopen north of the present town of Lewes on the Lewes Creek. There were about 30 settlers, all of them men. They built a wooden fort, planted crops, and started to look for whales in the bay. They also made friends with the Indians. Everything was going well. Then one day an Indian ran off with the metal coat of arms that the Dutch had nailed to a pole. A coat of arms is a symbol, like a flag. It had great meaning to the Dutchmen. The Indian wanted it because it was made of metal. When the Dutch saw that their coat of arms was missing they became angry and demanded that the Indian who had stolen it be punished. Some of the Indians became so frightened that they killed the Indian who had taken the coat of arms and brought his head to the Dutch.

You can see by now that the Lenni Lenape and the Dutchmen did not understand each other's customs very well. Because of this misunderstanding, a little problem became a BIG problem. The Dutch were very sad that the Indians had punished the thief so severely. They did not know that many of the Indians thought that the punishment was unfair and blamed the Dutch. One day while the Dutch settlers were in their fields tending to their crops, the angry Indians sneaked up on the fort. There was one large building in the fort. A big dog guarded the entrance to the building. The Indians overcame their fear of the dog and shot it full of arrows

Indians attacking Fort Zwaanendael

before it could bark and warn the settlers. Then they killed all the settlers.

The next year David Pietersen De Vries came to Zwaanendael from Holland. He was to be the new leader of the colony. He found the colony destroyed and the fort burned. An Indian told him the sad tale of what had happened. De Vries hoped to rebuild the colony, but he was not able to do so. The whaling venture had not produced much whale oil, so the Dutch were not willing to spend more money on Zwaanendael. De Vries sailed up the bay into the river. He was very impressed with what he saw. He wrote in his journal that "This is

Courtesy of Ned. Hist. Scheepvaart Museum

DAVID PIETERSZ DE VRIES. 1502–?

David Pietersen De Vries
Courtesy of The Historical Society of Delaware

a very fine river and the land all beautifully level, full of
groves of oak, hickory, ash, and chestnut trees, with
many wild grape vines growing upon them. The river
has a great plenty of fish—perch, roach, pike, and
sturgeon—as in our Fatherland.''

The Fatherland of David Pietersen De Vries was, of
course, Holland. His hometown was Hoorn. Even though
the colony that De Vries tried to establish in Delaware

The Zwaanendael Museum in Lewes, Delaware
Courtesy of State of Delaware, Division of Historical and Cultural Affairs

failed, we still remember him as a brave man who had a good plan. In Lewes, Delaware, there is a museum called the Zwaanendael Museum. It looks like the town hall in Hoorn, Holland. It was built to honor this early Dutch settlement. There are many interesting exhibits in the museum about the history of the Lewes area.

CHAPTER FOUR
The Swedish and Dutch Colonies

IN 1610, ONE year after Henry Hudson discovered the Delaware Bay, an English captain, Samuel Argall, sailed into the bay. Argall came from Jamestown, Virginia. The English had settled Jamestown three years before, in 1607. Samuel Argall named the Delaware Bay for the governor of Virginia, Thomas West, a

Thomas West, 3rd Lord De La Warr
Courtesy of The Virginia State Library

King Gustavus Adolphus of Sweden

nobleman whose title was Lord De La Warr. The Dutch did not adopt this English name. They called the Hudson River the North River and they called the Delaware River the South River.

Sweden was another European country that was interested in the Delaware region. Can you find Sweden on the map? You will see that it is very far north in a part of Europe that is called Scandinavia. Sweden is on a peninsula that faces two great seas, the Baltic Sea to the east and the North Sea to the west. Sweden had good seaports but not many traders. In the 1600s most of the Swedish people were farmers.

Sweden was an important country because it had a big army led by its king, Gustavus Adolphus. Gustavus Adolphus won many battles and conquered new lands for Sweden. Gustavus Adolphus wanted to make Sweden an important trading country like Holland. A Dutch merchant told the king that the best way for Sweden to develop trade was to settle a colony in the New World.

The Swedish government created a company, called the New Sweden Company, to establish a colony. He brought skilled Dutch sailors and traders to Sweden to

Queen Christina of Sweden, as a child
Photograph courtesy of The Historical Society of Delaware

"KEY OF KALMAR" (Kalmar Nyckel)
FIRST SWEDISH SHIP UP THE DELAWARE

The "Key of Kalmar" under the command of Peter Minuet made a landing near Lewes, Delaware in the middle of April 1638. She then sailed up the Delaware to what is now Wilmington. The spot where they landed was called "Paradise Point."

The *Kalmar Nyckel*
Courtesy of The Historical Society of Delaware

help plan the colony. Then in 1632, before the colony got started, King Gustavus Adolphus was killed in a battle. His daughter, Christina, became queen. Christina was only six years old when she became queen. Can you imagine a first grader becoming the head of a country! A council of Swedish nobles actually ruled in her name until Christina reached the age of eighteen. This Council supported the old king's plan for a colony in the New World.

In November 1637, two ships sailed with settlers from Sweden to America. The two ships were the *Kalmar Nyckel* and the *Vogel Grip*. *Kalmar Nyckel* means "the key of Kalmar." Kalmar is a city in Sweden. *Vogel Grip* means "griffen," which is a bird. Peter Minuit led the group of settlers. Minuit knew that no European country had settled colonists on the west bank of the Delaware River. He also knew that the Delaware River bordered rich land. That is why he chose this river as the best place for the New Sweden colony.

In March 1638, after several stormy months at sea, the *Kalmar Nyckel* and the *Vogel Grip* sailed up the

"The Landing of the Swedes" by Robert Shaw
Courtesy of The Historical Society of Delaware

Delaware River into a smaller river. They named the small river the Christina for their young queen. The colonists landed on the Christina River at a place where rocks had made a natural dock. The rocks can still be seen in the Christina River. They are now part of a park in Wilmington called The Rocks. There is a monument in the park that was later built to celebrate the landing of the Swedes.

Only a small group of Swedes wanted to come to New Sweden. There was still plenty of farmland at home and the new colony seemed far away and very strange. Therefore, the New Sweden Company had to recruit other settlers. It was against the law in Sweden to shoot wild animals on a nobleman's estate or to clear land for farming by burning down forest trees. Sometimes poor people had no choice but to do these things in order to eat. If they got caught they might be sent to New Sweden. Probably one half of the settlers who came to New Sweden were Finns, whose country, Finland, had been conquered by Sweden. One of the colonists in New Sweden was a black man named Anthony, who came from Africa. He was the first black man in Delaware.

Most of the Swedish and Finnish settlers were poor people, but they knew how to live in the wilderness. They had lived in or near large forests before. They knew how to survive in the forest with only a few tools. They could make their own furniture and kitchen utensils from wood. They ate on wooden bowls with wooden spoons. They knew how to build a house from logs with just an ax. They did not need nails or saws.

Fort Christina Park in Wilmington, at The Rocks. The monument, representing the *Kalmar Nyckel*, was made in Sweden in 1938 to celebrate the 300th anniversary of the Swedish landing. Courtesy of the Delaware Division of Historical and Cultural Affairs.

The Swedes and Finns built the first log cabins in America. A visitor who saw the colony said that the Swedish houses were "built of round logs with the door so low that it is necessary to bend down when entering. As the colonists had no windows with them, small loopholes served the purpose, covered with a sliding board which could be closed and opened." The colonists pushed clay into the cracks between the logs on both sides of the walls. The fireplaces were made from granite rocks found on the hills.

The Swedish settlers also built a star-shaped fort near The Rocks called Fort Christina. They built Fort Christina of logs and dirt. None of the fort survives today but we do have a drawing of it. The fort protected the colonists from Indian attacks. To make their defenses as strong as possible, the Swedes built the fort next to marshlands. Why do you think they did that? They also put a cannon on top of the walls of the fort. They hoped that the loud booms from the cannon would frighten the Indians if they attacked.

Fortunately for the Swedes, the Indians were friendly. Peter Minuit met with the Lenni Lenape chiefs, and the Indians agreed to sell the Swedes all the land along the Delaware River from the Smyrna River in the south to the Schuylkill River in the north. The Swedes paid for the land with presents. The Indians also gave Peter Minuit beaver skins and beads to show that they wanted to trade with the Swedes.

In spite of this friendly agreement, there were troubles ahead for the Swedes. The Dutch did not want to share the fur trade with the Swedes. They protested that New Sweden was built on land that belonged to Holland by right of Henry Hudson's discovery. In addition to this, the Indians and the Swedes had different ideas about land ownership. The Swedes, like all Europeans, believed that owning a piece of land gave the owner the right to keep other people from using it. The Indians did not think this way. To them land was free to all, like the air and the water. The Indians thought that they had agreed to share the land with the Swedes. The Indians did not realize that they had given up the right to hunt, plant, and fish on the land that they had sold.

The New Sweden colony was small, but the people worked hard to make it a success. They sent furs to Sweden and planted tobacco to sell back home. The Swedes and Finns tried to live as they had lived in Sweden and Finland. After the first years, women came to the

N.C. Wyeth's portrait of Johan Printz
Courtesy of The Delaware Art Museum

settlement. Soon the colony had families and children. The settlers imported farm animals to the colony to provide food and to help with the work. The ships that brought new colonists also brought horses, oxen, cows, and pigs. These animals were new to the Delaware Indians. The Swedes and Finns learned from the Indians how to grow corn and other native American crops. But they also planted wheat, rye, barley, and other crops from home.

The leader of New Sweden was the governor. The governor was in charge of keeping order in the colony. The governor who served longest in New Sweden was Johan Printz. Johan is the Swedish name for John. Governor Johan Printz was a remarkable man. He was a very stern governor who demanded obedience and hard work from the colonists. He was well educated and had had many interesting experiences as a cavalry officer in

Arrival of Gov. Printz at Fort Christina
Courtesy of The Historical Society of Delaware

the Swedish army. The most remarkable thing about Governor Printz was his size. He was a huge man who weighed nearly four hundred pounds. Can you imagine how happy his horse was when he quit the cavalry to become a colonial governor!

Governor Printz arrived in New Sweden in 1643. All the colonists gathered to see their new governor. The sounds of a trumpet and drum roll aroused the people's expectations. Then their new governor appeared. The people were amazed by his size and by his strict military look. They held their breaths as the governor marched down the gangplank. The gangplank sagged under his weight. Although the people feared Governor Printz, he was a good governor who kept the little colony going in spite of many troubles.

Today there are two reminders of the Swedish colony in Wilmington. One of them is the park at The Rocks with its stone monument that shows the *Kalmar Nyckel* and various events in the history of New Sweden. About one block from the park is a church called Holy Trinity or Old Swedes Church. The Swedes built the church in 1698. It is one of the oldest churches in the United States. The man responsible for building Old Swedes was the Reverend Mr. Eric Bjork, a Lutheran minister from Sweden. He built the church close to the Christina River because many Swedish families came to church by boat.

OLD SWEDES' CHURCH. - BUILT IN 1698.

Courtesy of Hagley Museum and Library

The main part of the church is built of Brandywine granite, a blue-gray stone found along the Brandywine River. Inside the church, the floor is made of brick. The most important object in the church is a beautiful but plain pulpit carved from black walnut. This pulpit, like many others in colonial days, has a canopy that is like a little roof over the minister's head. A wooden dove representing the Holy Spirit hangs from the canopy. The dove is a symbol often used in Swedish Lutheran churches. Another interesting item in the church is the model of the *Kalmar Nyckel*. The model was a gift from Sweden. The church is still in use today and you can visit it to see where the early colonists worshipped. A graveyard surrounds the church. Many Swedish families are buried there.

As the years went by, relations between the Dutch and Swedes became worse. The governor of New Netherland was Peter Stuyvesant. Like the Swedish governor, Johan Printz, Peter Stuyvesant was a soldier. He had a wooden leg because he had lost one of his legs in a battle. He lived in the town of New Amsterdam. Peter Stuyvesant believed that the Swedes had no right to be living on the Delaware River. He wanted to stop the Swedes from buying furs from the Indians.

In 1651 Peter Stuyvesant decided to challenge the Swedes. He sent eleven ships and a small army to the South River. The Dutchmen built a fort a few miles south of Fort Christina at the present site of New Castle. They called it Fort Casimir. Governor Printz was very angry, but he wisely did nothing to provoke the Dutch. Governor Printz knew that the Dutch had more soldiers in America than he had. In 1654, after eleven years as governor of New Sweden, Governor Printz went home to Sweden.

A new governor, named Johan Rising, came to New Sweden. When Governor Rising sailed up the Delaware River, he saw Fort Casimir and ordered his soldiers to attack it. The nine Dutch soldiers who were in the fort quickly surrendered. Governor Rising thought that he had won a big victory. But he was wrong. When Peter

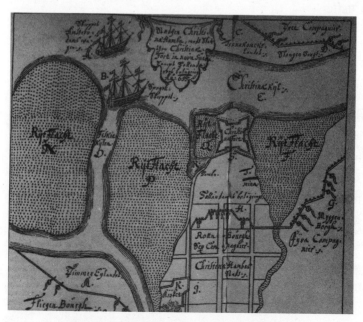

Fort Christina under siege by the Dutch, 1655
Courtesy of The Historical Society of Delaware

Stuyvesant heard about the attack, he decided to go to war against New Sweden.

In August 1655, Governor Stuyvesant sailed from New Amsterdam to the South River with seven ships and 317 soldiers. When the Swedes in Fort Casimir saw the size and power of the Dutch fleet, they surrendered. The Dutch then sailed upstream to Fort Christina. Some of their soldiers removed cannons from the ships and set them up behind the fort so that they could bombard Fort Christina from two sides. Governor Rising recognized that the fort was surrounded. He surrendered New Sweden to the Dutch. The Dutch promised that the Swedish and Finnish settlers who wanted to stay could keep their land.

The Dutch ruled the South River for only nine years, from 1655 until 1664. During this short time they built a town next to Fort Casimir. They called the town New Amstel. The town they founded is now called New Castle.

Fort Casimir and New Amstel
Courtesy of The Historical Society of Delaware

New Amstel was a trading post where the Indians sold furs and the farmers sold tobacco. The Indians and farmers traded their goods for cloth, iron tools, and liquor. The Dutch built a church in New Amstel, and their governor lived in the town. The houses of New Amstel were built of wooden planks and logs. They had fireplaces and chimneys of brick. The houses stood in neat rows along the town's streets. By 1660 several hundred people lived in New Amstel. The Dutch also rebuilt their old community at Zwaanendael and re-named it Hoerekil.

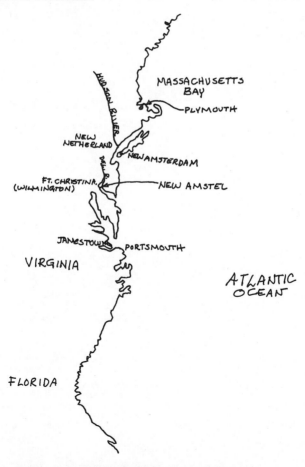

Map showing English and Dutch colonies (c.1655)

The Dutch now had control of both the Hudson River and the Delaware River. They had built the towns of New Amsterdam at the tip of Manhattan Island and New Amstel on the west bank of the Delaware River. But Dutch power was not secure. The English had established colonies both north and south of New Netherland. Thousands of English people lived in Massachusetts. That is where the Pilgrims had established Plymouth in 1620. There were other English colonies in Virginia and Maryland. The English wanted to conquer New Netherland and make it part of their American colonies.

UNIT TWO

DELAWARE UNDER THE ENGLISH

CHAPTER FIVE

The English Conquest

A FEW YEARS after the Dutch attacked the Swedes, the English attacked the Dutch. An English fleet sailed into the harbor at New Amsterdam and demanded that Peter Stuyvesant surrender New Netherland to England. Peter Stuyvesant wanted to fight, but the other Dutch leaders knew that the English were too strong. The tough old peg-legged governor had to surrender.

King Charles II of England sent part of the English navy to America. His brother James, the Duke of York,

The fall of New Amsterdam, from a painting by J.L.G. Ferris
Courtesy of The Historical Society of Delaware

King Charles II of England
Courtesy of The Historical Society of Delaware

James, Duke of York
Courtesy of The Historical Society of Delaware

was Admiral of the Fleet. King Charles promised to give New Netherland to his brother if the fleet could capture the colony. While James stayed in England, he sent some of his ships to attack New Netherland. The English captured the Dutch capital, New Amsterdam, and renamed it New York to honor the duke. They also captured New Amstel, which they renamed New Castle. Just as the Dutch had allowed the Swedes and Finns to keep their land, so the English allowed the Dutch, Swedes, and Finns to stay in their settlements along the Delaware Bay and River. Not everyone was happy with the new government, however. The Calvert family of Maryland believed that the settlements along the Delaware belonged to them.

In 1632 the King of England had given Cecil Calvert, also known as Lord Baltimore, a charter to establish a colony in America. The Calvert family founded Maryland to be a safe colony for English Catholics. England was at that time a Protestant country. People who did not go to the official Church of England were often put in jail. Maryland attracted both Catholic and Protestant settlers from England.

The Delaware Charter
Courtesy of Delaware State Archives

Cecil Calvert, 2nd Lord Baltimore, with a map of Maryland in his hand,
and his grandson by his side
Courtesy of Enoch Pratt Free Library. Reproduced by permission.

According to the Calverts' charter, Maryland's eastern boundary was the Delaware Bay and River. But the charter also said that Maryland could not include land that had already been settled by Europeans. When Cecil Calvert died, his son Charles became the leader of Maryland. Charles Calvert believed that the Dutch settlements at New Amstel and Hoerekil were on his land. When Calvert's fellow Englishmen conquered the Dutch he expected them to give him the land on the Delaware Bay and River. But the Duke of York did not do so.

Calvert tried to use military force to seize Hoerekil. Once a troop of Maryland soldiers came to the village of Hoerekil and claimed it in Calvert's name. The soldiers said that they had orders to kill all the farm animals there and to burn down all the buildings. The people of Hoerekil pleaded against this cruel action. But the Maryland soldiers burned the village anyway. Fortunately

Marylanders burning Hoerekil

one barn refused to burn. The soldiers believed that this was a sign from God. They stopped trying to burn it and let pregnant women and women with small babies move into the barn to keep warm.

This raid was only the worst of several raids that the Marylanders made against the settlement at Hoerekil. These raids showed that Calvert was very determined to claim his right to the land on the Delaware Bay. But the Duke of York still refused to give the land to Calvert. Since the Duke was the King's brother it was difficult for Calvert to win his point, but he never stopped trying to win.

In 1681 there was a big change in land ownership along the Delaware River and Bay. King Charles II created a new colony that he gave to William Penn. The colony was called Pennsylvania, which means "Penn's Woods." William Penn and his heirs were to be the leaders of Pennsylvania, just as Cecil Calvert and his heirs were the leaders of Maryland. These leaders encouraged settlers to come to their colonies by giving them land. The settlers then paid taxes called quitrents to the leaders.

William Penn was a member of a religious group called the Society of Friends, or Quakers. The Quakers, like the Catholics, did not conform to the Church of England and were persecuted for their beliefs. The Society of Friends did not have priests, preachers, prayer books, or hymns. Quakers met in very simple buildings that they called meeting houses, not churches. They believed that God speaks to people through an Inner Light that is within each person. During the Quaker Meeting everyone sat silently. People spoke only when they received the prompting of the Inner Light.

The Quakers' views set them apart from other Englishmen. They did not believe in social ranks and would not call anyone by a title, such as "Mister," "Sir," or "Your Majesty." They called everyone by the familiar

William Penn, in Quaker dress
Courtesy of The Historical Society of Delaware

pronouns "thee" and "thou." A Quaker would not bow or remove his hat as a sign of respect toward someone of higher social rank. A Quaker would not even remove his hat before the King. Quakers believed that all problems between people could be resolved through friendly understanding. That is why Quakers refused to go to war or to fight other people for any reason.

If you look at a map of the middle Atlantic states you will see that Pennsylvania's eastern boundary is the Delaware River. In the 1660s roads were very poor. The best way to travel was by ship. William Penn realized that without the Delaware Bay and River no one could get to his colony. That is why William Penn asked the Duke of York to give him the lands that the duke held on the Delaware south of Pennsylvania. In 1682 the duke agreed to give William Penn the land that he had won from the Dutch on the west bank of the Delaware Bay and River. This land was separated from Pennsylvania by the part of a circle called an arc, measured 12 miles from New Castle. The 12 mile arc still marks the boundary between Delaware and Pennsylvania.

In October 1682 William Penn and a group of Quaker colonists sailed up the Delaware River on the ship *Welcome*. William Penn first set foot on his new land at New Castle. Representatives of the Duke's government presented Penn with various symbols of ownership—a key to the fort, a piece of soil, a twig, and a cup filled with river water.

By 1682 the land that the Duke gave to William Penn had already been organized according to the customs of English government. The English created three counties along the Delaware Bay and River. Each county had its own court that was responsible for keeping order and settling arguments. When William Penn came to Delaware, New Castle County already had its name. William Penn named the other two counties Kent and Sussex for counties in England. All together they were known as the "Three Lower Counties on Delaware." The court for New Castle County met in the town of New Castle. The court for Kent County met in what became the new town of Dover on the St. Jones River. The court for Sussex County met in Lewes, which was the new name for the old Dutch settlement of Hoerekil.

One of the most important things that William Penn did was to create a new town on the Delaware River in Pennsylvania. He named the new town Philadelphia, which means "city of brotherly love." Philadelphia attracted many settlers and quickly became an important market town. Within a few years Philadelphia was attracting more trade than New Castle. Philadelphia became the largest and most important town in the Delaware River Valley.

William Penn treated the Indians fairly. Quakers believed that fair treatment prevents arguments and that without arguments there can be no wars. Penn met with the Indian chiefs in Philadelphia and made a treaty with them. He told them that he would pay for their land if they were willing to sell it to him. Many of the Indians sold land to William Penn and moved farther west. Most of the Indians who were still in the Three Lower Counties on Delaware moved west too. The Indians could no longer hunt, fish, or farm very well because the settlers had taken the best land. Most of the fur-bearing animals, such as beavers, bears, and foxes, had been killed in this area, so the Indians had to move west to continue the fur trade. The Three Lower Counties on Delaware now belonged to the European settlers.

William Penn's treaty with the Indians
Courtesy of The Historical Society of Delaware

CHAPTER SIX
William Penn and Delaware

IN THE LAST chapter we learned how William Penn came to be the leader of the Three Lower Counties on Delaware. Do you remember the names of the counties? We learned that in 1682 William Penn established the new trading town of Philadelphia on the Delaware River in his province of Pennsylvania. We learned that the Indians were leaving the Delaware River Valley and moving west into the forests. All of these developments showed that the land along the Delaware Bay and Delaware River was no longer a frontier. Towns were growing; farms were being established; and government was becoming more orderly.

Two ideas guided William Penn in creating a government for his two colonies. The first idea was that he wanted the people in his province of Pennsylvania and in his Lower Counties to get along together. The second idea was that he wanted the settlers to be part of the government. As leader, Penn could have made all the laws himself, but he believed that the people should also take part in making the laws. In his government William Penn created an assembly that would meet once a year. The people in Pennsylvania and in the Three Lower Counties elected representatives to the assembly. The assembly was responsible for voting on the laws. The assembly was divided into two houses, or parts, that met and voted separately. One house of the assembly was called the Legislative Council. The other house was called the House of Assembly. Together they made up the *General Assembly*. Not everyone could vote for representatives or serve in the assembly. Voters had to prove that they owned some land or had some money. Members of the assembly had to own land or have money. The members of the two houses of the assembly were elected to represent the three counties in Pennsylvania and the Three Lower Counties. In this way, both colonies had an equal voice in the government.

William Penn hoped that the assembly would make the people of the two colonies feel that they were part of one government. But it did not work out that way. Most people who lived in Pennsylvania were Quakers. They came from England and Wales. The people who lived in the Lower Counties came from many different countries including Sweden, Finland, Holland, and England. Although a few of them were Quakers, most were not.

The Quakers from Pennsylvania and the non-Quakers from the Lower Counties might have gotten along well in peaceful times. But the years from 1688 until 1714 were not peaceful. During that time England was at war with France. Most of the fighting took place in Europe, but some of it reached the Delaware Bay. Back in those days, governments increased the size of their navies in wartime by letting trading ships become ships of war. These ships were called *privateers*. They roamed the seas attacking, capturing, or burning the ships of the country they were fighting. Privateers did not really behave very differently from pirates.

Attack of privateers

"So The Treasure Was Divided" by Howard Pyle
Courtesy of The Delaware Art Museum, Howard Pyle Collection

In the 1690s French privateers attacked towns and
farms in Sussex County. In 1698 a privateer attacked
Lewes. Fifty sailors from the French ship captured the
town and stole belongings from the people. They took
anything of value that they could carry away, including
bed linens, clothing, farm animals, weapons, and table-
ware. They even took the town carpenter because they
needed his skills. Privateers and pirates also attacked
isolated farm houses. They seized ships and terrorized
the people who lived on or near the Delaware Bay. The
pirates and privateers liked the Delaware coast because
it offered many little rivers where they could hide. Two
famous pirates, Captain Kidd and Captain Blackbeard,
both sailed in Delaware waters. Legend says that Captain Kidd buried treasure near Rehoboth.

The assemblymen representing the Lower Counties
wanted Penn's government to do something to stop the
pirates and privateers. They wanted to set up many
cannons in Lewes to protect the town. They wanted to
organize a militia, or army of citizens, who could fight
pirates and privateers.

The Quaker assemblymen from Pennsylvania refused
to vote for a militia or for weapons because they did not

believe in fighting. The Delawareans pointed out that the Pennsylvanians might feel differently about defense if they lived close to the ocean. The pirates and privateers did not attack towns as far north as Philadelphia, so the Pennsylvanians were not threatened. The two sides could not agree.

The *population*, that is, the number of people in Pennsylvania was growing faster than the population in the Lower Counties. Soon Pennsylvania would demand more representatives in the assembly. The people who lived in the Lower Counties believed that their interests would be forgotten. In 1701, the assemblymen from the Lower Counties told William Penn that they wanted to have their own assembly, separate from that of Pennsylvania. William Penn did not want to agree to separate assemblies, but he saw that the people of the two colonies were not getting along together. Sadly, he agreed to

New Castle Court House
Courtesy of The Historical Society of Delaware

let the Lower Counties have their own assembly.

This decision was important in Delaware's history because it meant that Delaware would not become a part of Pennsylvania. After 1704 Pennsylvania and Delaware each had its own assembly. The assembly of the Lower Counties met each year at the courthouse in New Castle. You can visit the courthouse and see what it looked like when the colonial assembly met there.

The Lower Counties might remain separate from Pennsylvania, but could they remain separate from Maryland? Remember that the Calverts, the proprietors of Maryland, believed that the Lower Counties belonged to them. Charles Calvert and William Penn could not agree on the boundary line between their two colonies. They went to a court in England to settle the dispute. Believe

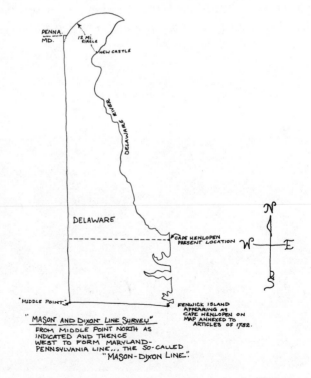

Map showing settlement of Maryland-Delaware border dispute
Note 12-mile arc.

it or not, the case took nearly 70 years to resolve! By the time the English court reached its decision, both William Penn and Charles Calvert had died. Their heirs in the Penn and Calvert families received the court's decision.

The argument put forward by the Calvert family was based on the charter for Maryland that King Charles I gave to Cecil Calvert in 1632. Remember that the charter said that Maryland would go eastward as far as the Delaware Bay and River and include all land that was not already settled by Europeans. This charter seemed to make Delaware part of Maryland. But William Penn knew his history! He knew that the Dutch had settled Zwaanendael one year before the King had given Calvert his charter. The court agreed with Penn and gave the Lower Counties to him.

Today you can see a historic monument in Lewes that explains the importance of the short-lived Zwaanendael settlement. The inscription says: "That Delaware exists as a separate commonwealth is due to this colony." Now when you see this monument you will know why that is so.

Two English surveyors, Charles Mason and Jeremiah Dixon, then drew the boundary lines between Maryland, Pennsylvania, and Delaware. The Mason-Dixon line sep-

Zwaanendael Monument in Lewes
Courtesy of Delaware State Archives

arates northern Maryland from southern Pennsylvania. This line later became famous in American history because it was the line between the North and the South.

Before they marked the Maryland-Pennsylvania boundary, Charles Mason and Jeremiah Dixon drew the boundaries between Maryland and the Lower Counties. Their boundary line still separates Maryland and Delaware.

Mason-Dixon Boundary Marker
Courtesy of Delaware State Archives

The boundary lines around Delaware are easy to understand if you look at a map while you read this explanation.

1. Delaware's eastern boundary is the Atlantic Ocean, the Delaware Bay, and the Delaware River. It is Delaware's only natural boundary. But it is affected by the twelve mile circle as you will see in Number 4.

2. Delaware's southern boundary was established by the English court that settled the Penn-Calvert controversy. It is a straight line that runs from the middle of Fenwick Island in the east to a point midway on the Delmarva Peninsula between the Atlantic Ocean and the Chesapeake Bay.

3. Delaware's western boundary is the one that was surveyed by Charles Mason and Jeremiah Dixon. It is a straight line that runs north from the midpoint on the peninsula to the boundary line between Pennsylvania and Maryland. Mason and Dixon had a difficult time surveying this line because it ran through undeveloped wilderness land. They placed stone boundary markers every mile along the route. Recently Delaware's western boundary was re-surveyed using much more modern instruments than Mason and Dixon had. The modern surveyors found that Mason and Dixon's survey had been very accurate. They were never more than a few feet wrong.

4. Delaware's northern boundary is the twelve mile circle that was measured from the courthouse in New Castle to separate Pennsylvania from the Three Lower Counties. The twelve mile circle extends not just north but in every direction. This means that all of the Delaware River within twelve miles of New Castle is part of the state of Delaware. Below twelve miles, Delaware's boundary with New Jersey lies in the middle of the Delaware Bay and River.

CHAPTER SEVEN
Life in Colonial Delaware

IN THE LAST two chapters we learned how the English came to rule the Three Lower Counties on Delaware. In this chapter we will learn how the colonists lived and worked in the Lower Counties during the early 1700s. As you read, try to imagine what it must have been like to live in Delaware more than 250 years ago.

While William Penn and Charles Calvert argued over who owned the Lower Counties, both leaders granted large pieces of land to settlers. Many of those who settled in Kent and Sussex counties came from Maryland. They received grants of land from Calvert. Fortunately for them William Penn was willing to accept Calvert's grants of land in Kent and Sussex counties.

Maryland farmers raised tobacco as their major crop. Growing tobacco required many workers. The farmers could not do all the labor themselves, so they bought

Slave and overseer in tobacco fields

54

slaves from Africa. They bought the slaves from slave ships that came to ports along the Chesapeake Bay. The ships were overcrowded, and many of the African people died or became weak during the long voyage.

The Africans had been captured and taken from their homes in West Africa. They were used to farming at home and so knew how to raise crops and harvest them. But they were not used to living under the control of Englishmen. English was a foreign language to them. They found many English ways peculiar. Their religious beliefs were very different from those of the English. Worst of all, they had no freedom in America. They were completely under the control of their masters. Some masters were cruel. All masters made their slaves work very hard.

When farmers from Maryland moved to Kent and Sussex counties, they brought their slaves with them. This is how slavery became a part of farm life in the Lower Counties.

Tobacco was one of the major crops raised in Kent and Sussex counties. But farmers there raised many other crops as well. They planted grains such as corn, barley, and wheat. They also kept cattle and hogs. The people who lived on the farms ate many of the crops they grew, but they always tried to grow some crops to sell. With the money they earned from selling their crops, they bought manufactured goods, slaves, or more land. The biggest market for farm crops was Philadelphia. Small sailing boats, called shallops, took the crops up the Delaware River to Philadelphia.

Craftsmen lived in Philadelphia and in the towns in the Lower Counties such as New Castle and Lewes. *Carpenters* were craftsmen who worked with wood. They built houses and made tools and furniture. They knew which kinds of wood were best for each job. The wood used most often to build houses was pine that had been sawed into planks at a sawmill. Roofs were made

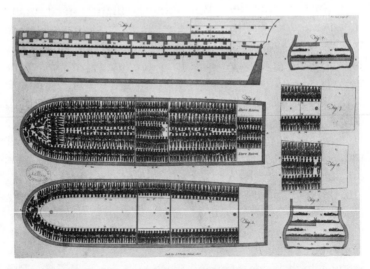

Africans were crowded into every possible space on the slave ships that
brought them to America.
Courtesy of The Historical Society of Pennsylvania

Loading Flour on a shallop
Courtesy of Hagley Museum and Library

from short cedar boards called shingles. Tools and furniture were made from hardwoods like maple, cherry, and oak. Most of these woods could be found in the forests of the Lower Counties. Many pine trees and cedar trees in Sussex County were chopped down and sold for lumber.

Another important craft was *masonry*. Masons were skilled at laying bricks and building stone walls. The stone came from the banks of rivers in the Piedmont Plateau. The Brandywine River especially had many stones. Bricks were made from clay. The clay was put into a mold in the shape of a brick. The brick was then baked in an oven until it became hard.

Smiths worked with metals. The most important metal was iron. The settlers imported much of their iron from

Blacksmith with apprentice

England, but they also dug iron ore in the Lower Counties. Iron ore was put in a furnace that made it so hot that it melted. The dirt and other metals could then be removed and the iron could be shaped. Blacksmiths hammered the hot iron into useful objects, including horseshoes, parts for harnesses, door hinges, cooking pots, and hoes.

All of these crafts were difficult to learn. It took a lot of practice to know how to make a chair, construct a stone wall, or forge a horseshoe. Boys who wanted to learn these crafts became *apprentices*. An apprentice studied in a craftsman's shop, not in a school. Apprenticeships started between ages nine and twelve. The apprentice usually studied for seven years. During that time, the apprentice stayed with his master and had to obey him. The apprentice learned by doing very simple jobs for his master. He watched how the craftsman did his work. As the apprentice learned, he became able to do more and more of the work himself. Finally, the apprentice had learned enough to become a craftsman on his own.

In addition to farmers and craftsmen, the other people most important to the colonial economy were merchants and sea captains. The merchants lived in the towns, particularly in Philadelphia. They bought wheat, corn, barley, tobacco, hides, lumber, and other products from the farmers. They sold these products wherever they could find a buyer. The most successful merchants owned ships. The ships took the products of Delaware River Valley farms to sell in faraway places where people needed them. The ships brought back goods that the colonists could not make or grow for themselves, such as fine cloth, coffee, tea, chocolate, and glass.

We know how some Delaware families lived during the 1700s from old letters, diaries, and legal documents that have been kept in the Historical Society of Delaware and in the State Archives. We know a lot about

one family, the Rodneys. The Rodney family owned
several big farms near Dover in Kent County. In the
early 1700s, Dover was a small town of about forty
houses. Most of the people of Kent County lived on big
farms far from their neighbors. They went to Dover to
attend church or to do legal business at the county court.

William Rodney came to Lewes from England in
1681 at about the time that William Penn acquired the
Lower Counties. In 1692 he moved to Kent County,
where he owned farm land. He married Sarah Jones.
She owned a farm that her father had given her in his
will. William and Sarah had six children, five sons and
one daughter. Several of the children died young. Only
their son named Caesar married and had children of his
own. One of William and Sarah Rodney's grandsons,
Caesar Rodney Junior, became a famous patriot during
the Revolutionary War.

William and Sarah lived on one of their farms and
hired other farm families to be *tenants* on their other
farms. Tenants were people who rented the property
where they lived. The tenants did not pay the Rodneys
with money but with a portion of the crops they grew.
The Rodneys also owned slaves. Sarah Jones Rodney
inherited some slaves from her father. These slaves are
mentioned by name in his will. Sarah inherited a girl
named Maria, who was probably her personal servant
and housekeeper. Maria may also have cooked for the
family. In addition to slaves, the Rodneys employed
servants from England who worked on their farms to
pay the cost of their passage to America.

The slaves, servants, and tenants did not do all the
farm work. The Rodneys' sons helped to plant and
harvest crops. But most of the time the Rodneys were
free to do other things. The Rodneys' sons loved many
outdoor activities. They fished and collected oysters in
the Delaware Bay. They also enjoyed hunting for turkeys and geese in the marshes. When the blackberry

Colonial gentry children at play with slave in attendance

bushes, cherry trees, and peach trees bore fruit, they collected fruit and berries to eat. The Rodneys often rode on horseback to visit other farm families. Sometimes the families that owned the big farms got together and amused themselves playing cards and dancing. One of the Rodneys' sons played the fiddle at the dances.

The Rodney children did not spend very much time in school. Caesar Rodney Senior wrote this in his diary:

When I wass about 13 years old I went to school 3 muneths but went no more for two years at which time I had forgot all I had learnt before then I went 4 mouneths tell I Could Read Prettey Well In the bible and write a Littel.

You can probably write better than Caesar Rodney Senior could because you have gone to school longer than he did. Can you pick out the words he misspelled?

There were few schools in the Lower Counties in the early 1700s. Some parents taught their children at home. Sarah and William may have helped their children learn to read, to write, and to do arithmetic. Children who were apprentices sometimes learned these skills from their masters. Sometimes groups of parents hired a teacher to teach their children. Children could also learn to read at church. The ministers taught children to read the Bible and to memorize prayers and religious creeds. The Rodneys belonged to the Church of England. They went to Christ Church, Dover. The Reverend Mr. Crawford, who was the minister at Christ Church, probably taught the Rodney children to read the Bible. We know that the Rodneys were friendly with Mr. Crawford because Caesar Rodney Senior married Mr. Crawford's daughter, Elizabeth.

Christ Church, Dover
Courtesy of the artist, Isabella M. Kast

Early 18th-century silver tankard
Courtesy, The Henry Francis du Pont Winterthur Museum

In 1708 William Rodney died. He left farm land to each of his children. To his wife, Sarah, he left several farms and his silver tankard, a silver porringer, and six silver spoons. A tankard is like a mug and a porringer is like a cereal bowl. Except for his farms, these pieces of silver were the most valuable things that William Rodney owned. They were probably made in England and imported to America.

Sarah Rodney was now a widow. Her husband, William, had been an important person in the politics of Kent County. He had been a county judge and a member of the General Assembly. Women could not vote or take part in politics in the 1700s. But Sarah Rodney could manage the family farms. She now owned several big farms, and she operated them herself.

Sarah Rodney raised many different crops on her farms. She sent wheat and tobacco by shallop to Philadelphia. She also sent pork, beef, butter, and corn to market. Her merchant in Philadelphia was a Quaker named Samuel Preston. Sarah Rodney and Samuel Preston wrote many letters back and forth to each other. Sarah Rodney told Samuel Preston which things she wanted him to buy for her in Philadelphia. She bought linen material for clothing, hats for her sons, and shoes for members of her family. She also bought coffee, a frying pan, nails, rugs, blankets, buttons, leather, parts for guns, chocolate, hoes, and lime juice. These were all products that were either made in Philadelphia or imported from foreign countries. Samuel Preston's job was to get the best prices for Sarah's farm products and to send her the goods she asked for.

At home Sarah had to manage her farms and be a good mother to her growing family. She also had to take care of slaves, servants, and her children when they became ill. There was a doctor in Dover, but he was not usually much help. Babies were born at home, often with only family members to assist. When people got

Early 18th-century silver porringer
Courtesy, The Henry Francis du Pont Winterthur Museum

sick they took homemade medicines. Home-nursing was a big job. Many people died of injuries and sicknesses that can be cured easily today.

We do not know exactly when Sarah Rodney died. We do know that she lived long enough to see the birth of her grandson, Caesar Rodney Junior, who was to become one of the most important Delawareans who ever lived.

CHAPTER EIGHT
Founding Wilmington

IN 1731 A man named Thomas Willing founded a town on the banks of the Christina River. Thomas Willing called his town Willingtown. He laid out streets in a grid pattern, just as the streets in Philadelphia were laid out, and advertised the sale of lots. Thomas Willing thought that Willingtown would attract settlers because it could become a port. But several years went by and few settlers came.

Then in 1735, William Shipley, a wealthy Quaker merchant, decided to move to Willingtown with his family. William Shipley lived in Pennsylvania. He persuaded several other Quaker families to move to Willingtown too. William Shipley and his friends built a market house where farmers could sell their crops to the townspeople. The town attracted settlers who had faith in its future growth.

The story of William Shipley's decision to move to Willingtown is very interesting. William Shipley's wife, Elizabeth, was a leader among the Quakers. She traveled by horseback to visit Quaker meetings and share her visions of God's will.

In about 1728, when the Shipleys were still living in Pennsylvania, Elizabeth Shipley had a strange dream. She dreamed that she was traveling through countryside she had never seen before. She rode to the top of a hill from which she saw a wonderful sight. She saw beautiful country below her. A wide river was glistening in the sun. Two other rivers flowed into it. One of them moved rapidly through rocky hills; the other moved slowly through flat land. These two rivers came together

Elizabeth Shipley's dream

and entered the big river. The land in the valley around these rivers was filled with green meadows and tall forests. A voice told her that she and her family would live in that valley some day.

When Elizabeth awoke, she told her husband William about her dream. William was a very practical man who did not believe in dreams. For a long time Elizabeth forgot about her dream. Then in 1735 she took a trip to the Lower Counties to visit Quaker meetings there. She had never been to the Lower Counties before. Her path

This Quaker Meeting House was built in Wilmington, Delaware, in 1817.
Courtesy of The Historical Society of Delaware

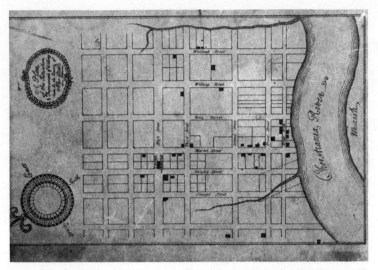

Willingtown now Wilmington, as it was laid out in the year 1736, showing the number of houses and where they stood at that time.

through New Castle County took her up a hill. What do you think she saw when she got to the top of the hill? There before her was the land she had seen in her dream! The large river of her dream was the Delaware River; the river flowing through rocky hills was the Brandywine River; and the river flowing through flat meadows was the Christina River.

Elizabeth Shipley could hardly wait to return home and tell her husband that her dream had come true.

William Shipley's house

Market house on market day

William agreed to go to see the land she described. When he came to the land of Elizabeth's dream he discovered that it had great possibilities for trade. The Christina River would make a good harbor, and there were many farms in New Castle County that could supply crops. That is why he bought land in Willingtown and moved his family there. Elizabeth Shipley's dream had come true.

Willingtown grew rapidly after the Shipleys moved there. In 1739 there were already 600 people living there. New houses of brick and wood were being built along the town's streets. William and Elizabeth Shipley built a big brick house. Thomas Willing built a dock along the Christina River. Both Thomas Willing and William Shipley built market houses where farmers came to sell butter, beef, corn, and other crops.

In 1739 the Penn family gave the town a charter. The charter allowed the town to hold markets and to organize its own government. The charter made one important change in Willingtown. It changed the town's name from Willingtown to Wilmington. The Penns named the town for the Earl of Wilmington, who was an important official in England.

Wilmington became a port for the farmers' goods. In 1740 William Shipley and some of his friends built a ship called *Wilmington* to carry these goods to the West Indies. The *Wilmington*'s first voyage took flour, beef, butter, and barrel staves to Jamaica. Barrel staves are pieces of wood shaped so that they can be put together to make a barrel. Well-made barrels have a very tight seal and do not leak. In the 1700s barrels were used to carry many goods that might leak, such as flour and rum. The craftsmen who made barrels were called *coopers*.

The farmers of New Castle County did not grow much tobacco. The crop that grew best in New Castle

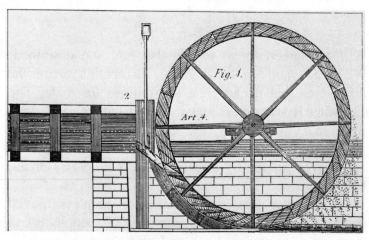

A Waterwheel in a mill
From Oliver Evan's *The Young Millwright and Miller's Guide*, Courtesy of Hagley Museum and Library

County was wheat. Wheat farming did not need as many workers as tobacco farming.

Wheat was ground into flour that was used to make bread. Bread was an important food for people in America and in the West Indies. The best way to carry wheat to the West Indies was to grind it into flour and ship it in barrels.

Flour was made by crushing wheat between two heavy round stones. In the 1700s, waterpower was used to make the stones move. Flour mills were built where there was a fast flowing stream of water. The stream of water hit a wooden mill wheel that had slats built into it. The force and weight of the water hitting the slats turned the wheel. The wheel was attached to the millstones and made them turn. The turning millstones ground the wheat into flour.

Flour mills were built throughout the Lower Counties. Some of the names of towns in Delaware like Milton and Milford tell us that they were built around mills. Most mills in the Lower Counties were small and did not provide much power, because most of Delaware is in the flat coastal plain where rivers and streams move slowly.

The best place for a mill is next to a fast-moving stream because the force of the water will produce a lot of power. The only place in Delaware where there are fast-moving streams is in the Piedmont Plateau. The Brandywine River is in the Piedmont Plateau. It is the best river in Delaware for turning waterwheels.

In 1742 a Quaker named Oliver Canby built a flour mill on the Brandywine River near Wilmington. Many farmers brought their wheat to Canby's mill. Oliver Canby bought the wheat from the farmers. He ground it into flour, put it in barrels, and sold it to merchants like William Shipley. The flour was then sent to market in the West Indies or in Europe.

Canby's mill was very successful. It increased the trade coming into Wilmington. Coopers came to the town to make barrels for the flour. Shipbuilders came to build ships to carry the flour across the ocean. They also built shallops so that farmers along the Delaware River in New Jersey and throughout the Lower Counties could bring their wheat to sell in Wilmington.

Soon other people built mills near Oliver Canby's mill. One of the most important millers was Joseph Tatnall. He owned several mills. The flour mills were located close together at the fall line of the Brandywine River. Remember that the fall line is the place where the Piedmont Plateau meets the coastal plain. The Brandywine moves down from the northern hills as a rapid-flowing rocky stream. At Wilmington it enters the coastal plain. From that point on, there are no rocks in the Brandywine. The water moves slowly with the tide from the Delaware River. Small ships can sail below the fall line in the Brandywine River.

"Brandywine Mills" by Bass Otis
Courtesy of The Historical Society of Delaware

The fall line was the best place on the Brandywine River for flour mills. Power to turn the waterwheels came from the fast-moving river to the north. Ships and shallops could sail from the Delaware River up the Brandywine to the fall line. Shallops brought wheat to the mills, and ships carried away the flour after it had been milled.

The Brandywine mills became famous in America, the West Indies, and Europe. The Brandywine mills produced very good flour and a lot of it. The flour trade made Wilmington into the biggest town in the Lower Counties. By the time of the Revolution nearly 2,000 people lived in Wilmington.

The millers who built and ran the mills were Quakers. They lived in stone houses close to the mills. Their little community was called Brandywine Village. It did not become a part of Wilmington until much later, in the 1860s. You can still see the millers' houses on Market Street in Wilmington, just north of the bridge over the Brandywine River. The houses were built in the 1700s from stone taken from the banks of the Brandywine. The mills were built of Brandywine stone, too. None of the original mills are standing today. The brick buildings that you can see on the north side of the Brandywine River near the bridge were mills built many years later.

This miller's house was built on Market Street just
before the Revolutionary War.
Courtesy of Hagley Museum and Library

UNIT THREE

DELAWARE GAINS INDEPENDENCE

CHAPTER NINE

The Disagreement with England

AFTER THE ENGLISH conquered the Dutch colonies on the Delaware River and the Hudson River, the English controlled all the land along the Atlantic coast of North America from Georgia to Maine. The English had thirteen colonies in America. These colonies were New Hampshire, Massachusetts (which then included Maine), Connecticut, Rhode Island, New York, Pennsylvania, New Jersey, the Three Lower Counties on Delaware, Maryland, Virginia, North Carolina, South Carolina, and Georgia.

Only one other nation had colonies north of Florida. That nation was France. The French established a colony on the St. Lawrence River in Canada. The capital of the French colony was Quebec City. Can you find Quebec on a map of North America? Notice that the St. Lawrence River leads inland to the Great Lakes. Now notice how close Lake Superior and Lake Michigan are to the Mississippi River.

During the period when the first colonists were settling on the Delaware River, French explorers paddled canoes up the St. Lawrence River to the Great Lakes. They discovered the Mississippi River, which is the greatest river of North America. The Indians called the

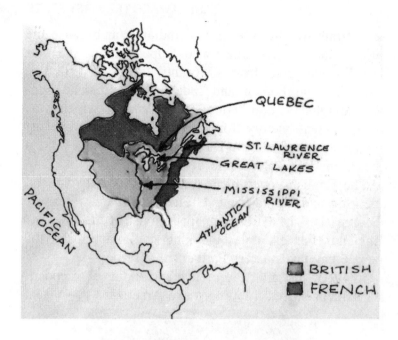

Map showing British and French colonies

Mississippi, "The Father of Waters." These explorers claimed all of the land around the Mississippi River, the Great Lakes, and the St. Lawrence as part of New France.

During the 1700s, England and France were often at war with each other. One reason they fought was for territory in North America. The French claims to land near the Great Lakes and along the Ohio River threatened the westward expansion of the English colonies.

In 1754 a young militia officer from Virginia named George Washington traveled through the wilderness to a French fort called Fort Duquesne to tell the French that they were on English soil. Fort Duquesne was on the Ohio River in Pennsylvania. The French fort was located where Pittsburgh is today. The French soldiers and the soldiers from Virginia fired at one another. This battle started the last of the wars between France and England for control of North America. The Americans called this war the French and Indian War because the French had Indian allies who helped them. The war lasted seven years, from 1756 until 1763.

During the French and Indian War, England conquered Quebec and won all of Canada, which was a very great victory for England. But the war cost England a lot of money. The English government wanted their American colonists to help pay the war debt.

The English government was made up of two parts, the king and the Parliament. The king at this time was George III. The Parliament made most of the laws for England. For example, the king could not make the people pay taxes unless Parliament agreed.

In 1765, just after the French and Indian War ended, Parliament passed a law to make Americans pay taxes.

King George III of Great Britain
Courtesy of The Historical Society of Delaware

The law was called the Stamp Act because it required the colonists to use official stamped paper for newspapers and legal documents such as wills, college diplomas, and deeds to land. An unstamped document would not be legal. The English government would make money from the sale of the stamps.

When news of the Stamp Act reached America, the people in all of the thirteen colonies were very angry. They believed that they had already helped England defeat the French. They also believed that England had no right to tax them. They believed that the Parliament in England only had the power to tax the people of England. They believed that only their own elected colonial assemblies could tax them. This principle was

A British tax stamp of 1765
Courtesy of The Library of Congress

best expressed in the saying, "No Taxation without
Representation." This saying means that people should

Caesar Rodney
Courtesy of the Architect of the Capitol

have the right to choose those who have the power to tax them.

News of the Stamp Act alarmed the Three Lower Counties. People in the Lower Counties refused to use the stamps. They sent two delegates to a meeting in New York to protest the Stamp Act. This meeting was called the "Stamp Act Congress." One of the delegates was Caesar Rodney Junior of Kent County. He was the son of Caesar Rodney Senior and grandson of Sarah and William Rodney. The Lower Counties' other delegate was Thomas McKean, a lawyer from New Castle County.

The Stamp Act Congress told Parliament that it had made a big mistake in trying to tax the colonists. Parliament repealed the Stamp Act, but Parliament still believed that it had the right to tax the colonists. In 1767 Parliament passed a new tax act called the Townshend Duties. This act put a tax on things that the colonists imported from England such as glass, paper, lead, tea, and paint.

John Dickinson, a lawyer who owned several farms in Kent County, published newspaper articles against the English tax. Dickinson said that the English tax was unfair and wrong. People in all thirteen colonies read Dickinson's articles, and he became famous. Today you can visit his farm in Kent County, south of Dover. You can walk through his house and barn and see how a wealthy farmer lived in those days.

The American colonists stopped buying English goods, which hurt the English economy. Parliament agreed to remove all of the Townshend Duties except for one—the tax on tea. In 1774 the English decided to sell tea in America at a cheap price. The leaders of Parliament believed that the Americans would buy the tea because tea was a very popular drink in America. Then the Americans would pay the tax and Parliament would prove its right to tax the colonists.

But the American colonists did not buy the tea. In

Boston, colonists disguised as Indians boarded the ship that brought the tea from England and threw the cartons

Engraved by T.B.Welch from a painting by G.Stuart.

THOMAS McKEAN

Thomas McKean
Courtesy of The Historical Society of Delaware

of tea into the harbor. This act was called the "Boston Tea Party." Another tea ship bound for the Delaware River did not dare to land. The Boston Tea Party made leaders in Parliament and King George III very angry. Parliament passed laws to punish the people of Boston. The English government closed the port of Boston and put the English army in charge of the government of Massachusetts.

The people who lived in the Lower Counties and in the other American colonies felt sorry for the people in Massachusetts. Caesar Rodney, the speaker of the Assembly in the Lower Counties, helped to organize meetings in all three counties to protest the English laws. Delawareans agreed to collect money to help the people of Boston. They also agreed to send delegates to a special Continental Congress representing all thirteen colonies. The Congress was to meet in Philadelphia to protest England's punishment of Boston.

The Lower Counties chose three delegates to represent them at the Continental Congress in Philadelphia. The delegates were Caesar Rodney, Thomas McKean, and George Read. George Read was a lawyer in New Castle. He was a leader in the colonial assembly.

John Dickinson House
Courtesy of State of Delaware, Division of Historical and Cultural Affairs

George Read
Courtesy of The Historical Society of Delaware

In Philadelphia, Rodney, McKean, and Read met delegates to the Congress from the other colonies. They met George Washington from Virginia, John Adams from Massachusetts, and many other colonial leaders. When Congress was not in session, the delegates often ate together at the City Tavern, the biggest tavern in Philadelphia.

While Congress was meeting in Philadelphia, the people of Massachusetts were preparing for war against the English soldiers. Farmers and craftsmen organized militia units and learned to be soldiers. They were called "Minute Men" because they were prepared to stop their work at any minute to go fight. On April 19, 1775, the English soldiers marched from Boston to the town of Concord, Massachusetts, to destroy the militia's gunpowder and weapons. The Minute Men gathered to stop the English. Shots were fired in the towns of Lexington and Concord. Both Massachusetts militia men and English soldiers were killed.

News of the fighting at Lexington and Concord soon reached Philadelphia. The Congress decided to organize an American army made up of men from all of the colonies to fight the English. They made George Washington the general in charge of the American army. The Revolutionary War had begun between England and the thirteen colonies.

Redcoats and Massachusetts Militia at Lexington
Courtesy of The Historical Society of Delaware

CHAPTER 10

Delaware in the Revolutionary War

THE REVOLUTIONARY WAR was very important in the history of America. All thirteen American colonies fought for independence from England. The thirteen colonies became states. They formed a new country called the United States of America. During the Revolutionary War, the Three Lower Counties on Delaware became the Delaware State.

When the war with England began, men in Delaware joined militia companies to fight the English army. Some Delawareans joined a regiment created by Congress. They became soldiers in George Washington's American army. The first leader of the Delaware Regiment was Colonel John Haslet. He was a doctor, born in northern Ireland, who lived in Dover.

The Delaware Regiment was among the best trained units in the American army. It was also one of the few units in the army that had military uniforms. The uniforms that the Delaware regiment wore were very handsome. The soldiers wore blue coats with white vests and light brown pants. They had tall hats made of black leather. The words "Liberty and Independence" were written on their hats. These words became Delaware's official state motto. You still see "Liberty and Independence" on Delaware's state seal and state flag.

The Delaware Regiment fought in many battles during the Revolutionary War. After Colonel John Haslet died in the battle at Princeton, New Jersey, two other men served as the regiment's leaders. They were Colonel David Hall and Captain Robert Kirkwood.

Not everyone in Delaware wanted to fight against England. Some people thought that Delaware should

A Delaware soldier in The Revolutionary War
Courtesy of The Historical Society of Delaware

remain loyal to England. The Loyalists wanted to work out the problems with England in a peaceable way. The *patriots*, who were the people who favored the war, called the loyalists *Tories*.

Most of Delaware's Loyalists lived in Sussex County. Their leader was a man named Thomas Robinson, who owned a big farm. Thomas Robinson tried to organize the Loyalists to stop the Revolution. He failed because Congress sent soldiers to Sussex County to fight the Loyalists. Thomas Robinson escaped to an English ship that was in the Delaware Bay.

Another Delaware Loyalist was a man born in England named Cheney Clow. He lived in Kent County. Cheney

Clow built a wooden fort west of Dover. The patriots marched to his fort, but Clow and his friends ran away without fighting. Many of the Loyalists were later captured. To punish them, the patriots made some of them join the American army.

During the Revolutionary War, the Congress in Philadelphia served as our national government. After the fighting started, many Americans wanted to declare the colonies independent of England. But some feared that America was not ready for independence. In May 1776 Congress asked the colonies to establish new governments independent of England.

Delaware assembly debating crisis with England

On June 15, 1776, the Assembly of the Lower Counties met in New Castle. Caesar Rodney was the Speaker of the Assembly. Thomas McKean told the members of the Assembly that Congress wanted the colony to separate from England. The assemblymen voted to do this. From now on the Lower Counties would not obey any English laws. They would write a new constitution for their government. Every year on June 15 there is a celebration in New Castle to honor that famous day. It is called "Separation Day."

On Separation Day the Lower Counties were separated from England. Delaware also separated from the Penn family and from any remaining ties to Pennsylvania. To make their separation from Pennsylvania clear, the assembly gave up the name Three Lower Counties on Delaware. The counties were no longer somebody else's lower counties. They were their own state—the State of Delaware.

On July 2, 1776, less than a month after Delaware's Separation Day, the Congress in Philadelphia voted to accept a Declaration of Independence of all thirteen colonies. All the Congressmen had to vote on the Declaration. Caesar Rodney was at his house in Dover on July 1 when a message came from Philadelphia to tell him that the vote on independence would be the next day. Rodney immediately set out for Philadelphia. He traveled along the dark, unmarked roads all night, through thunder and lightning storms.

Caesar Rodney's ride
Courtesy of The Historical Society of Delaware

When Caesar Rodney arrived in Philadelphia the next morning, he must have been very tired and dirty from his trip. Still wearing his riding clothes, he rushed into

Caesar Rodney's arrival at Independence Hall
Courtesy of The Historical Society of Delaware

the building (now called Independence Hall) where Congress was meeting. The other delegates were very happy and excited when Rodney declared his vote for independence.

Two days later, on July 4, 1776, the delegates to Congress accepted a document written by Thomas Jefferson of Virginia called the "Declaration of Independence." Thomas McKean, Caesar Rodney, and George Read all signed the Declaration of Independence for Delaware.

The Declaration of Independence was a wonderful statement of the aims of the new nation. The Declaration said that "All men are created equal." It said that the purpose of government was to give everyone the right to "Life, Liberty, and the Pursuit of Happiness." These were the goals that the delegates of all thirteen of the original United States of America agreed to work to achieve. They are still the goals of our country. They are not easy to achieve, and we do not always live up to them. Every generation of Americans must work to make these goals come true. They give our country, and our state, meaning and purpose.

On July 4, 1776, the thirteen colonies became the United States of America. But the new country still had to win the war against England to be free. During the same summer that Congress declared our independence, the English fleet brought a large army of English troops and Hessian soldiers (from the province of Hesse in Germany) to New York City. George Washington's army fought the English in the Battle of Long Island. The Delaware Regiment fought very bravely against the English. The Delawareans did not run away even when the English soldiers outnumbered them. General Washington saw their courageous stand and cried out, "Good God! What brave fellows I must this day lose!"

In spite of such heroism, the Americans lost the Battle of Long Island. By December 1776, Washington's army had lost several other battles. The English occupied New York City and all of New Jersey. Washington escaped with his army across the Delaware River into Pennsylvania. It was the hardest time for the Americans during the Revolution. Many people thought the English would destroy Washington's army and capture Philadelphia.

At this critical time, militia units from Pennsylvania and Delaware marched to join Washington. One of those militia units was led by Thomas Rodney, Caesar Rodney's younger brother. As they marched through New Castle County, Thomas Rodney and his men saw many frightened people fleeing from Pennsylvania. When they arrived in Philadelphia the city was nearly deserted.

Thomas Rodney and his men were not so easily discouraged. They thought they could beat the English and Hessians. General Washington thought so, too.

On Christmas Eve, Washington put his men into boats.

Washington's Army crossing the Delaware River
before the Battle of Trenton
Courtesy of The Historical Society of Pennsylvania

The Americans crossed the Delaware River to attack the enemy at Trenton, New Jersey. Thomas Rodney said that "the river was very full of floating ice, and the wind was blowing very hard, and the night was very dark and cold, and we had great difficulty in crossing."

Washington's army surprised and defeated the Hessian soldiers at Trenton. The army then moved on to Princeton and defeated the enemy soldiers there as well. General Washington showed that the Americans could beat the English and Hessians. All over the United States people became more hopeful that they would win the war.

Winning the war still did not come easily. In 1777 the English sent a large army by sea from New York to Elkton, Maryland. The English planned to march from Elkton to Philadelphia. General Washington moved his army to New Castle County to stop the English advance. Washington ordered one unit of his army under General William Maxwell "to be constantly near the enemy and to give them every possible annoyance."

On September 3, 1777, Maxwell's men stood waiting

Battle of Cooch's Bridge

for the English at Cooch's Bridge along the road from Glasgow to Newark, Delaware. When the enemy came in sight, Maxwell's soldiers opened fire on them. The English fired back with muskets and cannons. Then they charged with their bayonets. The outnumbered Americans withdrew. The Battle of Cooch's Bridge was the only battle of the Revolution fought in Delaware.

The enemy troops marched from Cooch's Bridge through Newark and headed toward Pennsylvania. General Washington's army was waiting for the English on September 11, 1777, when the enemy crossed the Brandywine River at Chadd's Ford, Pennsylvania.

The Battle of the Brandywine was one of the biggest battles in the war. People in Wilmington could hear the roar of the cannon fire as the sound traveled down the Brandywine Valley. They hoped that the Americans would win. The next day, when some English soldiers came into Wilmington, the people realized that the Americans had lost the battle.

The English expected to find flour in Wilmington to feed their army. But they were disappointed. George Washington had ordered that the flour be taken away. He also ordered the millers to hide their millstones. Why do you think he did that? The English stayed in Wilmington for several weeks. Then they joined their fellow soldiers in Philadelphia for the winter. George Washington and his army spent the cold winter living in log huts at Valley Forge, Pennsylvania.

The Revolutionary War continued for four more years. But no more battles were fought near Delaware. The English invaded the southern states of South Carolina, North Carolina, and Virginia. The Delaware Regiment fought in many battles in those states. Finally, in 1781, the Americans, with the help of France, defeated the English at Yorktown, Virginia. Parliament and King George III decided that they could not win the war in

America. In 1783 the English signed a treaty that declared the independence of the United States of America. The Revolutionary War was over.

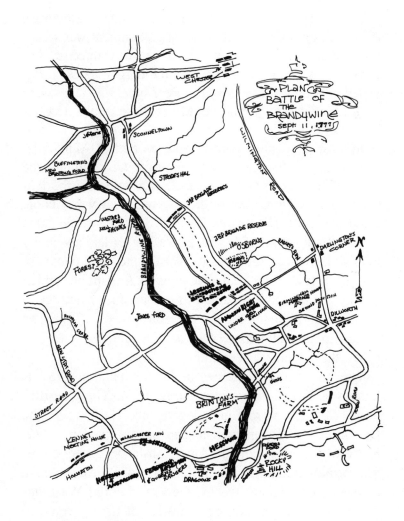

Battle of Brandywine—campaign map

CHAPTER ELEVEN

How Delaware Became the First State

AFTER THE REVOLUTIONARY WAR ended, Delaware faced hard times. The national government was weak. Each state was free to do whatever it wanted to do. Little states like Delaware feared the bigger states. Delawareans bought many goods in Pennsylvania. They were afraid that Pennsylvania would tax these goods as England had done.

In 1786 delegates from five states met at Annapolis, Maryland, to discuss how to improve trade among the states. Three delegates from Delaware attended the Annapolis convention. Two of them were the lawyers George Read and John Dickinson. The third Delaware delegate was Richard Bassett. He was also a lawyer and a wealthy man who owned farms in New Castle and Kent counties.

Only a few states sent delegates to Annapolis, which is why the delegates decided to call another meeting, to be held in Philadelphia in the summer of 1787. The Philadelphia convention was to consider ways to improve the national government.

The convention that met in Philadelphia in 1787 is known as the *Constitutional Convention*. The Constitutional Convention met in Independence Hall, where the Declaration of Independence had been signed in 1776. Some of the most famous American leaders were there. The printer Benjamin Franklin, now an old man, was a delegate from Pennsylvania. General George Washington of Virginia was chosen chairman of the convention.

The *Constitutional Convention* was the most important meeting in American history. It created the Consti-

The Constitutional Convention
Courtesy of Independence National Historical Park

John Dickinson
Courtesy of The Historical Society of Pennsylvania

tution of the United States. The Constitution, written in 1787, is still the law that governs our country today.

Delaware sent five delegates to the Constitutional Convention. George Read, the lawyer from New Castle, and his friend John Dickinson were the most important delegates from Delaware. The other Delawareans were Richard Bassett, Jacob Broom, and Gunning Bedford Junior. You know that Bassett was a lawyer and a wealthy farmer. Jacob Broom was a businessman from Wilmington, and Gunning Bedford Junior was a young lawyer who lived in New Castle County.

The Convention met all summer through the hot weather. The delegates had many decisions to make about the new national government. The most difficult problem was to decide how much power to give to the small states and how much to give to the large states. Delaware's delegates wanted each state to have equal power in the national government. Big states, which had more people, thought this was unfair.

After much debate, the Convention voted on a

Gunning Bedford, Jr.
Courtesy of The Historical Society of Delaware

Richard Bassett
Courtesy of The Historical Society of Delaware

compromise to end the argument between the big states and the little states. A compromise is an agreement in which each side gives up something. The compromise that was put into the Constitution works like this: there are two houses in the national legislature, the Senate and the House of Representatives. Each state, no matter how large or small, has two Senators. But in the House of Representatives, the number of representatives from each state is based on the number of people who live in that state. The big states have many more representatives than the small states have.

In the compromise, both sides gained something and both sides gave up something. Delaware's delegates supported the compromise. They thought that it was fair to Delaware.

The men of the convention finished writing the Constitution of the United States in September 1787. Nine states had to *ratify* the Constitution before it could become the law. To ratify means to agree.

When the Delaware delegates returned home from Philadelphia, they told the people of Delaware about the new Constitution. Delaware's voters elected delegates to meet in Dover to decide if Delaware would accept the Constitution. In 1787 there were no state government buildings in Dover, so the leaders met in a tavern on the green in Dover. The woman who owned the tavern was named Mrs. Battell. Her tavern is no longer standing.

On December 7, 1787, Delaware's delegates voted to ratify the Constitution. Delaware was the first state to vote for the Constitution. Now you know why Delaware is called the "First State." Today we celebrate Delaware Day on December 7.

Pennsylvania and New Jersey ratified the Constitution soon after Delaware did. By the spring of 1789, enough states had accepted the Constitution for the new national government to begin. George Washington was elected the first president of the United States. The United States now had a strong central government.

The State House, Dover Delaware. 1787-1792

Courtesy of The Historical Society of Delaware

Delaware, The First State
Ratification of the Federal Constitution

The ratification of the Constitution at Battell's Tavern, Dover, on
December 7, 1787, by Robert Goodier
Courtesy of Bank of Delaware

INAUGURATION OF GEN. GEORGE WASHINGTON
AS THE FIRST PRESIDENT OF THE UNITED STATES OF AMERICA
AT FEDERAL HALL, WALL ST., NEW YORK, APRIL 30TH 1789.
PUBLISHED BY WILLIAM BLACKMAN, 74 FULTON STREET, N.Y.

Courtesy of The Historical Society of Pennsylvania

UNIT FOUR

DELAWARE IN THE NEW NATION

CHAPTER TWELVE
The War of 1812

IN THE LAST chapter we learned how the United States Constitution was written and why Delaware is called the First State.

The year 1789, when George Washington became the first president of our country, was important for another historical event—the beginning of the French Revolution. The people of France overthrew their king. A few years later a general in the French Army, named Napoleon Bonaparte, became the emperor of France.

England went to war against Napoleon. The war lasted from 1803 until 1815. Napoleon conquered many countries in Europe, but he could not conquer England. Remember that England is an island. The English navy was very strong and protected England from the French emperor.

The United States did not take sides. At first, American merchants liked the war because both France and England bought goods from American ships. But after a while the English began attacking American ships that were trading with France, and the French attacked American ships that were trading with England. Since the English had a bigger navy than the French had, the English attacked more American ships.

The United States government tried to stop these attacks. In 1807 President Thomas Jefferson imposed an *embargo* on American shipping. An embargo is an order to stop all trade. The embargo was supposed to punish both England and France. American ships had to return to their home ports, which made them safe from attack, but the merchants could not make any money. The embargo stopped the merchants of Wilmington and New Castle from sending flour and other products to other countries.

When James Madison became president of the United States in 1809, he tried another plan. Madison promised to trade with England if the English would respect America's shipping. He promised to trade with France if Napoleon would respect American shipping.

The English navy still captured American ships. Often they took sailors off American ships and forced them

"Impressment of American Seaman," by Stanley Arthurs
Courtesy of Chas. Scribners Sons

to join the English navy. This practice was called *impressment*. Americans became so angry at the arrogant English that they wanted to go to war. In 1812 the United States declared war against England.

Compared to the huge English navy, the American navy was small. But the Americans soon showed that they could defeat English ships. One of the first American victories came when Captain Jacob Jones and the U.S.S. *Wasp* defeated the bigger English ship *Frolic* in October 1812. Captain Jacob Jones was a native of Smyrna, Delaware. His family moved to Lewes when he was a boy. He studied to be a doctor, but he loved the sea so much that he became an officer in the United States Navy instead. The victory of the *Wasp* over the *Frolic* made Captain Jacob Jones a famous hero in the United States.

In 1813 the English navy blockaded the American coast. The purpose of a blockade is to stop shipping. The English sent large war ships to close up American harbors. An English fleet came into the Delaware Bay

The Wasp vs. *The Frolic*
Courtesy of The Historical Society of Delaware

Colonel Samuel Boyer Davis
Courtesy of The Historical Society of Delaware

and anchored near Lewes. The English ships blocked the channel from the Delaware Bay into the Atlantic Ocean. No American ship could sail in or out of the Delaware Bay.

The Delaware militia prepared for the possibility of an English attack on Lewes. The commander of the militia was Colonel Samuel Boyer Davis. Colonel Davis was a native of Lewes. He was a brave and able soldier.

Shortly after the English fleet arrived in the Delaware Bay, the commodore in charge of the fleet sent a message to Colonel Davis. The English asked the people of Lewes to sell them food, such as beef and vegetables. Colonel Davis refused to sell food to the English. He told them that it was against the law for Americans to help their enemies. The English threatened that if they did not get the food they would destroy the town.

Under Colonel Davis's leadership, the people of Lewes prepared to meet the English attack. The people built a fort out of trees and sand. Militiamen from other parts of Delaware came to Lewes to help with the town's defense. Guns and gunpowder were brought into the town.

On April 6, 1813, the English ships began firing their cannons at Lewes. The English kept up their bombard-

British bombing of Lewes

ment for twenty-two hours. They fired many cannon-balls. They also fired burning rockets that were designed to set fire to the town.

The militiamen in Lewes had only a few cannons to fire back at the English ships. There were not enough cannonballs in Lewes for them to keep up the fire for long. Fortunately, the people of Lewes discovered that the cannonballs being fired by the enemy were the right size for their own cannons. The boys of the town gathered up the cannonballs so that the militiamen could shoot them back at the English ships.

The bombardment was very exciting! There was the loud noise of the cannons. There was also the red glare of the burning rockets. Everyone in Lewes joined in to help keep up the fight. The women and girls cooked food for the soldiers. The men fought, and the boys collected cannonballs.

The most surprising thing about the bombardment was how little damage it did. Nearly all of the English cannonballs fell into a marsh that lay between Lewes and the bay. The rockets shot over the town and landed harmlessly in the fields beyond. One chicken was killed by a cannonball, but no houses were destroyed. A cannonball did hit one house but the house did not collapse. In fact, the "cannonball house" is still standing in Lewes today. Somebody in Lewes wrote a funny poem to describe the battle: "The commodore and all his men, shot a dog and killed a hen."

The English finally realized that their ships could not destroy Lewes. After nearly two days, they stopped the bombardment. The people of Lewes were very relieved. They were also very proud of themselves for bravely facing the English and not running away. Their town was safe, and no one had been hurt. Everyone praised Colonel Davis for his leadership. Even the English commodore sent a message of congratulations to Colonel Davis.

The Cannon Ball House in Lewes
Courtesy of The Lewes Historical Society

The end of the bombardment of Lewes did not mean that the English fleet would give up its blockade. The English fleet remained in the Delaware Bay during the summer and fall of 1813. The English captured some American ships and chased river shallops. Sometimes English troops got into barges and rowed to the shore to steal cattle and chickens. Some slaves ran away to join the English because the English promised them freedom.

When winter came, the English fleet sailed away and did not return to the Delaware Bay. In 1814 the English attacked Washington, D. C., and Baltimore, Maryland, on the Chesapeake Bay. During the English bombardment of Fort McHenry in the Baltimore harbor, Francis Scott Key wrote our national anthem, "The Star Spangled Banner." The "rockets' red glare" in the song refers to the same kind of rockets that the English had fired at Lewes the year before.

Commodore Thomas McDonough
Courtesy of The Historical Society of Delaware

In 1814 Commodore Thomas McDonough of St. Georges in New Castle County won an important victory against the English. Commodore McDonough led an American fleet that defeated an English fleet on Lake Champlain. You can find Lake Champlain on a map of the United States. It is in the northeast corner of New York State.

The war between England and the United States ended in 1815. President James Madison sent a group of Americans to Europe to meet with English political leaders. The two sides met in the city of Ghent in Belgium and signed a treaty of peace. One member of the American delegation was Senator James A. Bayard of Delaware. Senator Bayard lived in Wilmington. He knew that the war was hurting Delaware. That is why he was very eager to bring it to an end.

The news of peace reached Delaware early in 1815. People all over Delaware celebrated. In Lewes, especially, people fired guns, lit candles in their windows, and cheered the end of war. The militiamen were discharged from duty. Ships could sail wherever they wanted without fear of attack.

Delaware has not been attacked by an enemy nation since the War of 1812. We all hope that Delaware will never be attacked again.

James A. Bayard at the signing of The Treaty of Ghent
Courtesy of The Historical Society of Pennsylvania

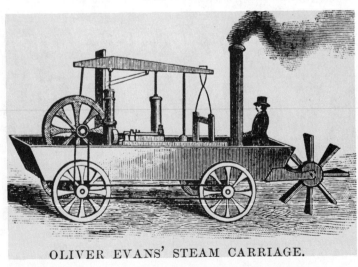

OLIVER EVANS' STEAM CARRIAGE.

Oliver Evans designed the Orukter Amphibolos to travel on land and in the water.
Courtesy of The Historical Society of Delaware

CHAPTER THIRTEEN
Industry and Transportation

THE YEARS FROM 1807 to 1815 brought many changes in Delaware. During these years new machines were invented. The machines brought about big changes in the way products were made. There was also a change in the way people did their work. During this time, the first factories were built in America. Some of these factories were in Delaware.

Do you remember what powered the flour mills in colonial Delaware? It was the power of water hitting a waterwheel. Water was now used to power many new kinds of machines. One of the most important new uses of waterpower was in making cloth from cotton and wool. Waterpower was also used to make gunpowder and paper. All of these products were made in Delaware.

In the factories, machines did most of the work in making things. Machines could usually do the work faster than people could. The machines did jobs that people found boring. A leader in the invention of machines was Oliver Evans.

When Oliver Evans was a boy in Newport, Delaware, he liked to experiment with machines. He once built a steam-powered machine that could move on land and in the water. He called it the "Orukter Amphibolos." The Orukter Amphibolos was an important invention, but it was too big and slow to be very useful.

The most useful of all of Oliver Evans's inventions was his improved machinery for flour mills. Oliver Evans made a series of leather belts to carry the wheat to the millstones. The continuously moving belts carried the heavy sacks of grain around the mill so that men did not have to carry them on their backs. Mills that used

A flour mill before Oliver Evans' inventions
Courtesy of Hagley Museum and Library

Evans's inventions needed fewer workers than did other flour mills. The flour millers on the Brandywine used Oliver Evans's inventions in their mills.

About one-half mile up the Brandywine River from the flour mills at Brandywine Village, Joshua and Thomas Gilpin built a paper mill in 1787. The Gilpins were Quakers from Philadelphia. In the Gilpin paper mill, rags were hammered into pulp. The pulp was mixed

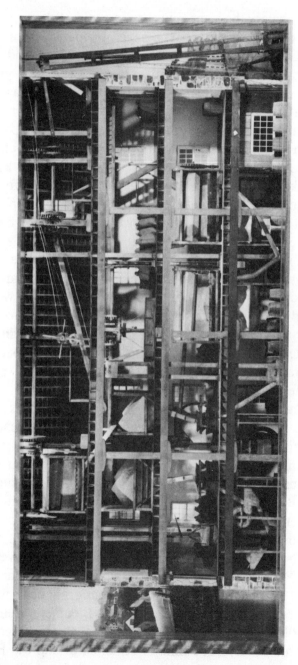

An Oliver Evans flour mill
Courtesy of Hagley Museum and Library

with water, then put into a wire mold. When the solution dried, it had become a page of paper. Not long after the Gilpins built their mill, a Frenchman invented a way to make a continuous roll of paper. The new process was much faster than the old way of making paper one page at a time. The Gilpins were the first paper manufacturers in America to use the continuous roll process.

Joseph Bancroft started a mill to make cotton cloth on the Brandywine River. Joseph Bancroft was an English Quaker. As a boy in England, he had learned from his uncle how to make cotton cloth. In 1824 Joseph Bancroft came to Delaware. He worked for another cotton maker until 1831, when he set up his own mill.

Joseph Bancroft's cotton factory became one of the biggest and most important companies in Delaware. The Bancroft Company hired many workers. The workers lived in rows of houses that the company built for them near the factory. Most of the Bancroft Mill buildings are still standing, but they are no longer used as part of a cotton factory. The workers' houses are now private homes.

Cotton factories were very noisy. The machines moved fast. Many workers were needed to keep the machines running properly. The cotton was spun on spinning machines and woven on big looms. In addition to the Bancroft Mills, there were several other textile mills on the Brandywine. Breck's Mill and Walker's Mill made cotton and woolen goods. These two mills are still standing on the property of the Hagley Museum.

The most famous mills on the Brandywine were the Du Pont Powder Mills at Hagley. The powder mills were founded in 1802 by a young French chemist named Eleuthère Irénée du Pont. Eleuthère Irénée du Pont had learned how to make gunpowder in France. He and his family had come to America during the French Revolution.

When Eleuthère Irénée discovered how bad American-

The Bancroft cotton mill
Courtesy of Hagley Museum and Library

made gunpowder was, he decided to build a powder mill. He chose to place his mill on the Brandywine River. His mills were far enough away from Wilmington so that if the powder blew up it would not kill the people in the town.

Eleuthère Irénée du Pont's powder mills made the best gunpowder in America. During the War of 1812, the mills sold powder to the American army and navy. The powder used by the Delaware militia in 1813 at Lewes to fire at the English ships came from E. I. du Pont's mills.

A powder mill was a dangerous place. The workers had to be very careful not to make sparks or light fires. The powdermen were not allowed to smoke while they worked! The workers' families lived in rows of stone houses near the mills in a village called Henry Clay Village. The du Pont family also lived in a large house near the mills.

All of the people who lived at Hagley participated in the life of the community. The powder workers' wives and children collected branches from willow trees. The willow branches were burned to make charcoal, which

Eleuthère Irénée du Pont
Courtesy of Hagley Museum and Library

was an ingredient in the powder. Eleuthère Irénée du Pont had four daughters. His daughters started a Sunday school to teach the children of the powder workers to read. Many of these children worked in cloth mills six days a week. Sunday was the only day when they could go to school.

Today you can visit the Hagley Museum and see what it was like to live at the powder yards in the early 1800s. You can walk through Eleuthère Irénée du Pont's house. You can visit the Sunday school. You will also see exhibits that show how gunpowder was made and a waterwheel that is still being turned by water from the Brandywine River.

The mills on the Brandywine River made northern Delaware one of the most important centers of manufacturing in the United States. The goods made in these mills—flour, paper, cloth, and gunpowder—were sent all over the United States and even to other countries.

"The Du Pont Powder Mills" by Bass Otis
Courtesy of Hagley Museum and Library

During the years from about 1800 until 1860, another big change was taking place in America: the improvement in transportation. In these years new types of transportation were created that allowed people and goods to move more quickly.

Can you imagine how slow travel was in the colonial days? The roads were not paved. Whenever it rained roads became muddy and rutted. Carriages and wagons could hardly move in some seasons of the year. The best transportation for heavy goods was sailing ships. But the ships hardly moved if the wind was not blowing, and they could only go where there were rivers, lakes, and oceans.

The first big improvement in transportation was called the *turnpike*. A turnpike was an improved road. People who used a turnpike had to pay a toll. The toll man's gate was a long pole, called a pike, that prevented people from entering the road without paying. After the

Workers' housing at Walker's Bank, Henry Clay Village
Courtesy of Hagley Museum and Library

people paid, the toll man turned his gate to let them enter. That is why these roads were called turnpikes. Turnpikes usually had a surface of crushed stone. Several turnpikes were built in New Castle County to connect Wilmington to other towns and cities. Some of these roads are still major roads today and are still known by their old names. If you live in New Castle County you have probably heard of the Philadelphia Pike, the Kennett Pike, the Concord Pike, the Newport-Gap Pike, and the Lancaster Pike.

The turnpikes made it easier for farmers to bring their grain to the mills at Brandywine Village in their farm

Farm wagon at turnpike gate

wagons. Inns were built along the turnpikes so that travelers could stop to get food for themselves and for their horses or stay overnight. Some of these old inns are still in use today as restaurants.

Another new way to travel was by *canal*. Americans began building canals after the end of the War of 1812. Canals were man-made waterways that connected a natural waterway at one end with another natural waterway at the other end. To make a canal, many men with shovels dug a long ditch wide enough and deep enough for a boat to move through it. When the canal was finished, the last dirt was dug out and water rushed in from the natural waterways to fill the canal.

One of the most important canals in the United States is the Chesapeake and Delaware Canal. It connects the Delaware River to the Chesapeake Bay. Construction began on the Chesapeake and Delaware Canal in 1824. It was completed in 1829. The canal runs 13.6 miles, all the way across Delaware. Many of the canals built during the 1820s are not in use any more, but the Chesapeake and Delaware Canal is busier than ever. It is now owned and managed by the United States Army Corps of Engineers.

The Chesapeake and Delaware Canal has been enlarged several times. Now large ocean-going ships can go through it. Many of the ships that use the canal today, like those that used it back in 1829, are going from Baltimore to Philadelphia or from Philadelphia to Baltimore. Look at a map that shows both Baltimore and Philadelphia. You will see that the Delmarva Peninsula lies between these two cities. Now find the Chesapeake and Delaware Canal on the map. Can you see why the ships use the canal?

A new invention that changed transportation was the steam engine. In 1807 Robert Fulton built a successful steamboat, called the *Clermont*, on the Hudson River.

Lock in the C & D Canal

Instead of sails, the steamboat had a steam engine that turned paddle wheels that moved the boat forward. Soon steamboats were being built at ports on the Delaware River. Many steamboats were built in Wilmington. Sailing shallops disappeared from the Delaware Bay and River because steamboats were faster.

Steam power was also used in another new type of transportation, the railroad. The first railroad in Delaware was the New Castle and Frenchtown Railroad, completed in 1832. The New Castle and Frenchtown Railroad crossed the Delmarva Peninsula just a few miles north of the Chesapeake and Delaware Canal. Like passengers on boats on the canal, most of the railroad's passengers were traveling between Philadelphia and Baltimore. Some were going an even greater distance between New York City and Washington, D. C. In either case, the passengers traveled by boat to New Castle or Frenchtown and then crossed the peninsula on the railroad.

In 1838 another railroad was completed through northern Delaware. This was the Philadelphia, Wilmington, and Baltimore Railroad, known as the P. W. & B. The P. W. & B. carried its passengers all the way from Philadelphia to Baltimore by train. It linked Delaware's major city, Wilmington, to the two biggest cities in the region.

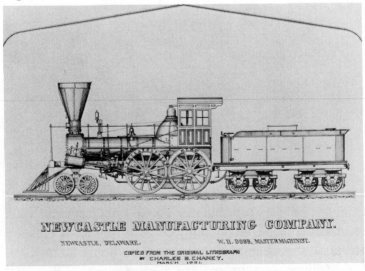

An early steam locomotive
Courtesy of The Historical Society of Delaware

During the 1850s another railroad, called the Delaware Railroad, was built from the P. W. & B. near Wilmington to southern Delaware. The Delaware Railroad ran along the western side of the state. It ran through Middletown, Clayton, and Harrington to Seaford. Later a branch of the railroad was built through eastern Sussex County to Lewes.

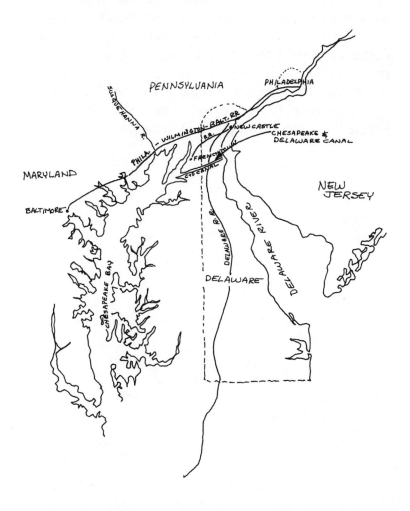

Map showing C & D Canal, New Castle & Frenchtown Railroad and Philadelphia, Wilmington, & Baltimore Railroad

The Delaware Railroad was very important to the farmers in western Delaware. Except for Seaford, which is on the Nanticoke River, western Delaware is not close to water transportation. The railroad allowed the farmers to get their crops to market. The railroad also helped towns to grow in the western part of the state.

These years after the American Revolution changed life for most people in Delaware. Craftsmen had once worked in small craft shops making things by hand. Now factories employed many workers and used big machines to make things. Towns and cities grew. Farmers could get their crops to market more quickly on steamboats and railroads. People could travel more easily. In the next chapter we will learn how these changes affected the lives of people in Delaware.

CHAPTER FOURTEEN
How Delawareans Lived

IN THIS CHAPTER you will learn what it was like to live in Delaware during the years from 1800 until 1850. You will learn about the religion of the people. As you read about life in the past, try to imagine how you would have lived back in those days.

During the American Revolution a minister named Francis Asbury began preaching in Delaware. Francis Asbury came from England. The religion he preached was called Methodism. The people who joined his movement were called Methodists. Methodists believed that it was very important to live a good life. They were against drinking liquor, gambling, and attending noisy parties. Instead, they spent their free time reading the Bible, attending church services, and helping people who were sick or in trouble.

Francis Asbury preaching

Barrett's Chapel
Courtesy of The Historical Society of Delaware

Francis Asbury was very sincere. After people heard him preach many became Methodists. By 1800 Methodists had built chapels throughout Delaware where they could meet to worship. Barrett's Chapel near Frederica in Kent County is the most famous Methodist chapel in Delaware. It is known as the "Cradle of Methodism" because it was where the Methodist church got started.

In 1805 the Methodists held a camp meeting in Kent County. This was the first religious camp meeting in Delaware. Many people came to the camp meeting and stayed for several days to pray together and hear the preaching. They slept in their wagons or in tents. The preachers stood on a wooden platform so that they could be seen and heard by all. The camp meeting was so successful that the Methodists decided to hold one every summer.

One person who joined the Methodists was William Morgan. He was a doctor who lived in Seaford. Dr. William Morgan said, after hearing the preachers, "I swapped my fiddle for a hymn book and determined to seek the Lord in earnest."

The Methodist church soon became the biggest religious group in Delaware. Black people as well as white people came to the camp meetings and joined the new Methodist churches.

Several black men from Delaware became famous Methodist preachers. The Reverend Mr. Richard Allen was born a slave near Dover. He and his master both became Methodists. Methodists believed that slavery was wrong. Richard Allen's master allowed Richard Allen to buy his freedom. Once he was a free man, Richard Allen drove a wagon to bring supplies to George Washington's army in the Revolutionary War. He was a friend of Francis Asbury, and he became a Methodist preacher. Richard Allen went to Philadelphia, where he started the African Methodist Episcopal Church.

Richard Allen
Courtesy of The Historical Society of Pennsylvania

Another important black Methodist leader was Peter Spencer. He belonged to Asbury Methodist Church in Wilmington. In 1800 the white members of Asbury Church ordered the black members to sit in the balcony. Peter Spencer led the black Methodists out of the church and helped them to found their own church, the African Union Methodist Church.

The church that Peter Spencer founded became the headquarters of black Methodist churches all over the Delmarva Peninsula. Every year on a weekend in August, black Methodists from Maryland, Delaware, and Pennsylvania gathered in Wilmington to celebrate an event called *Big Quarterly*.

Big Quarterly was the meeting of the African Methodist churches. But it was much more than that. Big

Peter Spencer
Courtesy of Mother A.U.M.E. Church, Wilmington

Quarterly was the one time each year when masters allowed their slaves to leave the farms and go to the city. Hundreds of free blacks and slaves came to Big Quarterly to see old friends. Everyone listened to sermons, heard the singing of gospel choirs, and ate picnic lunches. Big Quarterly was a very important occasion for black people from all over Delaware.

Religion played a big part in the lives of most people in Delaware during the years from 1800 to 1850. Religious groups tried to make life better for people in many ways. Religious groups helped to teach people in the state. They organized Sunday schools to teach children to read the Bible. But these schools only met one day a week, and there were not enough of them for all the children.

Delaware needed to build schools for all the children. In 1829 the Delaware legislature passed a law to create free public schools throughout the state. Students did not have to pay to attend the schools because the people's taxes paid for them. That is why the schools were

Willard Hall
Courtesy of The Historical Society of Delaware

Octagonal School
Courtesy of The Historical Society of Delaware

called free public schools. Under the law of 1829, the white children of Delaware had a chance to go to a free public school. In the school, they learned how to read, write, and do arithmetic. Black children did not get to go to school at that time.

The man who wrote Delaware's public school law was named Willard Hall. Willard Hall was a lawyer who came to Delaware from Massachusetts. In Massachusetts each town had a public school. Willard Hall wanted Delaware to have public schools, too. In 1823 Willard Hall became the judge of the United States District Court for Delaware. He devoted his spare time to starting public schools.

The schools in the 1800s were very different from the school you go to today. Each school was very small, usually only one room. There were no buses to take the children to school. The small schools were scattered all over the farm lands of Delaware so that the children could walk to them. One of the old schools that is still standing is the Octagonal School in Kent County, near Dover. The Octagonal School is now a museum. Visitors can see how children were taught 150 years ago.

In 1833 the state legislature chartered the first college in Delaware. The college was located in Newark, Dela-

"Old College," 1834, The original building of Delaware College, now the University of Delaware
Courtesy of The Historical Society of Delaware

ware. At first it was called Newark College. Later its name was changed to Delaware College. We know it today as the University of Delaware. For many years the college was only for young white men. The students had to pay a fee to attend the college. They also had to pay for their food and room. Poor boys could not afford to go to college in those days.

Most people spent a lot of time with their families. Whole families worked together in factory communities like Henry Clay Village. Other families farmed together. Farm women and their daughters cooked big meals several times a day to feed many people. Farm women also made clothing, soap, and other useful things. When the women had free time they got together to make quilts for members of their families. These quilts had very beautiful designs. Some of them are now in museums.

Sickness and accidents were common in those days. There were no hospitals. Families took care of sick people at home. The remedies for sickness had not improved much since colonial times. Most of the remedies did not help the patient very much. It was common to bleed sick people or to cause blisters to break out on their skin. People thought that bleeding and blistering would make the sick get well. Doctors could do little more to help the sick than could family members using home remedies.

Farming in Delaware changed more quickly than medicine. After the Revolutionary War an insect called the Hessian fly damaged wheat crops in Delaware. Farmers also noticed that crops were not growing well because the soil had lost its fertility. Some farmers left Delaware and went west to start new farms on the frontier. Some of those who stayed became poorer as their land continued to lose its fertility.

The most successful farmers in Delaware during the years from 1800 to 1850 were those who fertilized and planted new crops. Farmers who put lime, ashes, and other fertilizers on their soil got larger and better crops than those who did not.

Delaware farmers tried out several new crops. Some were successful. Others were not. During the period of the War of 1812, Americans could not get wool from England. Many Delaware farmers began raising sheep. But when the war ended English wool was imported again. The price of wool fell, and Delaware farmers gave up raising sheep.

Workers in a peach orchard
Courtesy of State of Delaware, Division of Historical and Cultural Affairs

Dairy farming and orchard crops were much more successful. When the Chesapeake and Delaware Canal was being built, a farmer near Delaware City, named Philip Reybold, began raising milk cows and peach trees. He first sold his milk, butter, and peaches to the men working on the canal. When the canal was finished, he shipped his products through the canal to Baltimore. He also used the new steamboats on the Delaware River to send fresh peaches to Philadelphia.

When other farmers saw the success of Philip Reybold, they began planting peach orchards, also. Delaware peaches became famous in Philadelphia and as far away as New York City. Philip Reybold showed other Delaware farmers how they could make use of the new rapid transportation to sell their crops in distant cities.

Every town and village had a general store. At the general store people could buy cotton, linen and woolen cloth, hats, needles, thread, boots, gloves, stockings, and even ready-made shirts and pants. The general stores

Interior of Thompson General Store, Thompsonville
Courtesy of The Lewes Historical Society

sold imported goods, such as tea, coffee, and chocolate. Stores also sold spelling books, rope, nails, knives, milk jugs, forks and spoons, horse collars, trunks, rugs, paper, blankets, bacon, molasses, crackers, cigars, soap, dyes, and tin stoves. The making, buying, and trading of all these many goods helped towns to grow and made life on the farm a bit easier than in the past. Women no longer spent long hours spinning and weaving at home. Instead, they bought ready-made cloth in the store.

After 1860, when the railroad was completed to southern Sussex County, no one in Delaware was far from rapid transportation. Those who lived on the eastern side of the state were close to towns such as Lewes, Milford, Dover, or Smyrna that were served by river steamboats. Those who lived on the western side of the state in towns such as Newark, Middletown, and Harrington were close to the railroad. Wilmington and Seaford had both steamboats and a railroad. Now people could visit each other more easily and could buy and sell things from farther away.

UNIT FIVE

DELAWARE IN A DIVIDED NATION

CHAPTER FIFTEEN

The First State Stays in the Union

YOU MIGHT THINK that better transportation would have tied the United States together more tightly. But this was not so. Soon after the War of 1812, Americans in the South felt a growing separation from Americans in the North. Part of the reason for this division was slavery. The northern states did not allow slavery. In the North, most people believed that slavery was wrong and should end. In the South, most white people believed that slavery was useful because they needed slaves to farm their big fields. The Mason-Dixon line divided the slave states from the free states.

Delaware was a slave state. The Dutch had introduced slavery into Delaware when they settled the area long ago. The English colonists had brought even more slaves to Delaware.

After the Revolutionary War, some farmers in Delaware freed their slaves. The Methodists and Quakers were against slavery. They convinced many people to free their slaves.

By 1860 slavery was dying out in Delaware. By then there were fewer than 1,800 slaves in the state. At the same time there were more than 90,000 whites and nearly 20,000 free blacks in Delaware. Slavery was still legal in Delaware, but it was becoming very uncommon.

Free blacks lived in all three Delaware counties. Some free blacks owned farms. Others were tenant farmers and farm workers. In Wilmington and other towns free blacks had many jobs. Some were skilled workers. Free black men were brickmakers, shipbuilders, carpenters, wagon drivers, sailors, cooks, and barbers. Free black men and women also worked as servants, nurses, and laundry workers.

Free blacks had some rights in Delaware. They could work where they wanted to for pay, and they could live where they wanted to. But many rights that white men took for granted were kept from black men. Black men could not vote or hold public office. They were not allowed to own guns. If they were found guilty of a crime, they might be kept as servants for a number of years.

Free blacks feared being captured by kidnappers and sold into slavery. During the 1820s, Patty Cannon and her gang were famous kidnappers. Patty Cannon lived at Reliance, Delaware, in Sussex County. Her house was on the line between Maryland and Delaware. If the sheriff from Sussex County came, she could run into the part of her house that was in Maryland, and he could not arrest her.

Patty Cannon and her gang captured free black people, tied them up, and took them by boat down the Nanticoke River. From the Nanticoke the boat went across the Chesapeake Bay to Virginia. Slaves were sold in markets in Virginia. There were no slave markets in Delaware.

In 1829, Patty Cannon was arrested when human bones were discovered in the ground near her house. She was put in the Sussex County jail in Georgetown. Legend says that before she was to be hanged she escaped from the jail. But this is unlikely. She probably died in her cell, perhaps from taking poison.

While Patty Cannon was taking black people south into slavery, other Delawareans were helping slaves to escape to the North. Thomas Garrett was a Quaker iron merchant who helped slaves to escape. He hid many slaves in his house in Wilmington. Then he put them under blankets or under hay in his wagon and drove them to Pennsylvania. Once a slave got to Pennsylvania, he or she was free because slavery was illegal in Pennsylvania. In 1850, the federal government passed the Fugitive Slave Law. Escaped slaves were no longer free anywhere in the United States. Many escaped slaves traveled farther north to Canada to freedom.

Harriet Tubman was a friend of Thomas Garrett. She was born a slave on the eastern shore of Maryland. She escaped from her master and came through Delaware to Philadelphia. Then she decided to go back down to Maryland to help the rest of her family escape. She was very brave. If her master had caught her, he would have punished her severely. Masters often beat their slaves with whips.

Patty Cannon gang kidnapping black person

Thomas Garrett
Courtesy of The Historical Society of Delaware

Harriet Tubman was not afraid because she believed that God was helping her. She found her family and led them out of slavery. The master chased after Harriet Tubman and her family with big dogs, but Harriet Tubman outsmarted the dogs. She took her family through a stream of water. The dogs could not keep the scent through water. She hid her family in marshes, barns, and forests. She also found out that there were people along the way in Delaware, like Thomas Garrett, who

Harriet Tubman leading slaves to freedom

were willing to help slaves to escape. These people hid the escaping slaves in secret hiding places in their houses or barns.

After Harriet Tubman got her family to safety, she returned to Maryland and southern Delaware many times to help other slaves to escape. She was never captured and never failed to lead the slaves to safety in the North.

The issue of slavery became more and more bitter in the United States. People feared that the nation would break in half. In 1860, Abraham Lincoln was elected president of the United States. Abraham Lincoln was against slavery. The southern states *seceded* from the United States. To secede is to leave the nation. The southern states started a new nation called the Confederate States of America. The United States had broken in half.

What was Delaware to do? The southern states hoped that Delaware would join the Confederacy. Men from the Confederate government came to Dover to talk to Delaware's General Assembly. The Confederates urged Delaware to leave the United States and join them. The members of the General Assembly told the Confederate representatives that the State of Delaware had been the first to join the United States. Delaware would be the last state to leave the United States.

Delaware stayed in the Union. Several other slave states refused to leave the United States also. They were Maryland, Missouri, Kentucky, and West Virginia. Slave states that remained loyal to the United States were called *border states*. They were on the border between the North and the South.

In the border states like Delaware people disagreed among themselves about the separation of the Confederate States. Some people thought that the United States should go to war to make the Confederate States come back into the Union. Others thought that the United States should accept the decision of the Confederate States to leave the Union. This debate divided people in nearly all the towns and villages of Delaware. It even divided some families. People who had been friends took opposite sides and refused to speak to their old friends.

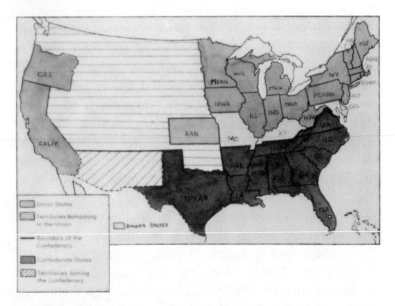

Map showing Confederate States, Union states, and Border states

Most of the people who lived in New Castle County were for the Union. They were close to Pennsylvania, which was a very pro-Union northern state. The people who lived near Seaford in the Nanticoke River area of Sussex County were the most likely to be for the Confederacy. Most of the slaves remaining in Delaware were in this area of the state. Sussex County was the part of Delaware closest to Virginia and the South. Kent County was divided on the question.

In April 1861 war broke out between the United States and the Confederate States when the Confederates fired on a United States fort, called Fort Sumter, in the harbor of Charleston, South Carolina. Charleston was a leading city of the Confederacy.

President Abraham Lincoln called on the people of the United States to restore the Union. He called on the loyal states to form armies to defend the nation's capital, Washington, D. C. Washington was located in a border area between Virginia and Maryland. Virginia joined the Confederacy. Maryland, like Delaware, was a slave state that remained in the Union. But many people in Maryland were for the Confederacy. Washington, D. C. was in great danger.

Soldiers from the northern states set out for Washington, D.C. They traveled through Wilmington on the Philadelphia, Wilmington, and Baltimore Railroad. People in Wilmington came down to the railroad station to cheer the soldiers and to give them food. But the soldiers were not so welcome south of Wilmington. Pro-Confederate people tried to stop the soldiers from reaching Washington by tearing up the railroad tracks in Maryland. When people in Wilmington heard about attacks on the Union soldiers in Maryland, they became very frightened.

The war that began in April 1861 did not end until April 1865. None of the battles of the Civil War was

fought in Delaware, but Delawareans did fight in the
Civil War.

Union soldiers marching through Wilmington

CHAPTER SIXTEEN
Delaware in the Civil War

DURING THE FOUR years of the Civil War about 12,000 men from Delaware joined the Union Army. About 500 Delawareans joined the Confederate Army. The Confederate soldiers from Delaware usually traveled to the South by boat across the Chesapeake Bay.

The soldiers in both armies had a hard life. During the summer they lived in tents. In the winter some built little log cabins. Whether in tents or in cabins, they were packed in close together. They could hardly move when they slept. Many soldiers got sick and some died without ever being in a battle.

Life in the army camps was often slow. The soldiers spent their time playing cards, reading, and writing letters home. Some of the troops from Delaware guarded railroads against Confederate attacks. It was important to keep the railroad lines running to bring soldiers and supplies to the armies. But guarding railroads was not very exciting.

The Union soldiers from Delaware fought in some of the biggest battles of the war. Many of these battles were fought no more than 100 to 200 miles from Delaware in northern Virginia and Maryland. The biggest battle of the war was fought less than 50 miles from Delaware, at Gettysburg, Pennsylvania.

Because Delaware was so close to the fighting, the Union built a hospital for sick and wounded soldiers in Wilmington. Many of the women in Wilmington volunteered to be nurses in the hospital. Women also raised money to support the hospital by making quilts and pies to sell.

CAMP BRANDYWINE.

Camp life in the Civil War
Courtesy of Hagley Museum and Library

The Union also had a prisoner of war camp in Delaware where they put Confederate soldiers captured in battle. The camp was located at Fort Delaware on Pea Patch Island. Pea Patch Island is a small island in the Delaware River near Delaware City. The fort had been built to guard the cities and towns along the Delaware River from enemy ships. Since the Confederates did not attack the Delaware River, the Union turned the fort into a prisoner of war camp.

Confederate prisoners were brought to the fort after every battle. Many of the prisoners died at the fort because of wounds or sickness. Mosquitos pestered the prisoners, and the prisoners did not get much to eat. In

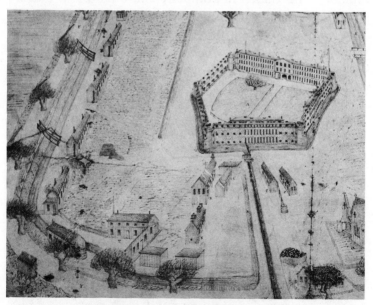

"Fort Delaware, 1864," by Max Neugas
Courtesy of The Historical Society of Delaware

the winter every two men had to share one blanket. Many of the prisoners were kept in the cold, stone dungeons of the fort. Others lived outside in little huts built on the marshy soil.

Some Confederate prisoners kept busy fishing in the

Delaware River, reading, or going to church services. Sometimes people who favored the Confederate cause brought them food and clothing. A few of the prisoners escaped by swimming to the Delaware shore at night. This was difficult even for a good swimmer because of the strong currents in the river. Those who made it usually found people who would help them to escape back to the South. Today you can visit Fort Delaware on Pea Patch Island. A small boat takes people to the island from Delaware City.

Manufacturers in northern Delaware made many things for the Union Army and Navy. Along the Brandywine, the Du Pont Company made gunpowder for rifles and cannon. The Bancroft Company and other cloth makers made material for tents and for soldiers' uniforms.

A number of industries in the city of Wilmington helped the war effort. During the Civil War, Wilmington was a center for carriage making, leather tanning, and shipbuilding. Carriage makers made horse-drawn

Confederate prisoners at Fort Delaware
Courtesy of The Historical Society of Delaware

ambulances and baggage wagons for the Union Army. Leather tanners made harnesses for the wagon horses, holsters for guns, ammunition containers, and shoes for the soldiers. The shipbuilders built steam-powered ships for the Navy. Wilmington was a very busy place during the Civil War.

In July 1863, the people of Wilmington stopped working for a few days. Word reached the city that the Confederate Army had marched into Pennsylvania. Everyone feared that the Confederates would march to Wilmington and destroy the city. Wilmington's workmen organized militia units and prepared to defend the city.

The Union Army fought the Confederate Army at the little town of Gettysburg, Pennsylvania. A big battle raged for three days. The Confederate Army finally lost and marched back to Virginia.

When word of the Union victory reached Wilmington

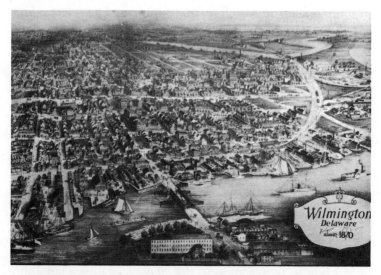

A bird's-eye view of Wilmington's industries during the Civil War
Courtesy of The Historical Society of Delaware

The Battle of Gettysburg
Courtesy of The Historical Society of Delaware

the whole city celebrated. People hung flags on all the houses and stores. Church bells rang. The fire companies led the people in a huge parade. Those who wanted the Confederacy to win kept silent.

During the war, President Lincoln published his Emancipation Proclamation. The Emancipation Proclamation freed all the slaves in the Confederate States. Delaware was not part of the Confederacy so the Emancipation Proclamation did not free the slaves in Delaware. The slaves in Delaware were not freed until after the Civil War when the Thirteenth Amendment to the United States Constitution made slavery illegal in the United States.

After four years of fighting, the Confederate armies surrendered in April 1865. Everyone in Delaware was relieved that the war was over and that the soldiers could come home. There were parades and celebrations in towns all over the state.

The joy at the end of the war lasted for only a few days. Then terrible news came from Washington, D. C. On the night of April 14, 1865, President Lincoln and his wife went to see a play in Washington. While President Lincoln was watching the play, a man named John Wilkes Booth shot the president and killed him.

1809 *Abraham Lincoln* 1865

From an original unretouched negative made in 1864.

President Abraham Lincoln
Courtesy of The Historical Society of Delaware

In Delaware and throughout the country people who had been celebrating only a few days before were now plunged into grief. The war was over, but the president who had led the Union to victory and had freed the slaves was dead. President Lincoln had promised to help "bind up the nation's wounds." The task of reuniting the nation would be very hard to accomplish without his leadership. Former slaves in Delaware and in the South did not know what sort of life to expect after slavery ended.

Celebration at end of war in Wilmington

CHAPTER SEVENTEEN

Black Delawareans after the Civil War

THE CIVIL WAR ended slavery but it did not make life much easier for black people in Delaware. The United States government promised that black people would become citizens with the same rights white people had, but for a long time this promise of equality was not kept.

Black men did not have the same rights white men had in Delaware. The state passed a law that made it almost impossible for black men to vote or to get elected to government in Delaware.

Black people hoped that they would now have the chance to go to school. Before the Civil War black children were not allowed to attend public schools in Delaware. After the war a group of people, blacks and whites, in Wilmington raised money to build schools for black people. With some help from the federal government, the group built one room schoolhouses in towns all over Delaware. They hired black teachers from Philadelphia to teach in the schools.

Black people of all ages flocked to the schools. Old men and women who had never been allowed to learn to read came to school. They sat beside their own children and grandchildren. They knew that learning reading, writing, and arithmetic makes a person free. Education frees the mind from ignorance. A few years later public education was finally opened to blacks, but it was still hard for them to get an education. The state did not allow black children and white children to go to school together. The state did not spend as much money on

The Georgetown school for black children in the 1890's
Courtesy of Delaware State Archives

Students and teacher in the Buttonwood School in New Castle in 1935
Courtesy of The Historical Society of Delaware

schools for black children as it did on schools for white children. Farmers and other employers kept many children, both black and white, out of school to work in fields or factories. Many children in Delaware did not learn much reading, writing, or arithmetic. Most black children had little chance to go to school.

Some young black people worked very hard to get a good education. In 1891, Delaware State College was founded in Dover. Delaware State College was the first school in Delaware to give black people a college education. The College taught young people to become farmers and teachers.

Another important school for blacks was Howard High School in Wilmington. Howard High School had many good teachers. Some students at the school went on to become doctors, professors, lawyers, businessmen, and teachers.

Young black teacher training blacks of all ages to read

Only a few black people in Delaware had the opportunity to study at Howard High School or at Delaware State College. Most black Delawareans lived in the country. A few owned their own farms. Most worked as farm laborers. Farm laborers were hired to help with farm chores. They helped to plant the seed and harvest the crops. They did not get paid very much for their hard work. Children worked in the fields with their parents. They had little time for play or for school.

Students and teachers at Delaware State College around 1900
Courtesy of The Historical Society of Delaware

Students studying in the library of Howard High School in the 1930's
Courtesy of The Historical Society of Delaware

Black caterer serving oyster dish at banquet

In the towns and cities black people continued to be employed in the jobs they had held before the Civil War. Some black men were wagon drivers. Others took care of horses in stables, or worked in factories. Some black men and women were servants and cooks in the homes of rich people. A few black cooks in Wilmington went into business to prepare fancy meals for big groups of people. These cooks were famous for their oyster and fish dishes. They bought the oysters and fish from other black men who caught fish and dredged for oysters in the Delaware River and Delaware Bay.

In the years from the end of the Civil War in 1865 until 1900, the way of life for black people did not change very much in Delaware. A few black people struggled to go to school and get good jobs. But most black people still had to work very hard and made very little money. Life did not change very much for them. It would take a long time for the promise of equal rights to become true.

Black people working on farm

UNIT SIX

DELAWARE IN A DEVELOPING NATION

CHAPTER EIGHTEEN
The Last of the Horse and Buggy Days

THE YEARS AROUND 1900 saw the last of the horse and buggy days in Delaware. New inventions like the telephone and the automobile, electric lights and electric trolley cars began to change the way people in Delaware lived. The city of Wilmington and its industries grew. People from European countries such as Poland, Italy, Russia, Ireland, and Germany came to live in Wilmington. They brought new cultures with them from their old countries.

In the years around 1900 the railroad was the most important means of transportation in Delaware. The railroad was very important to farmers. One farmer in Sussex County who made good use of the railroad was John G. Townsend Junior. As a young man, John G. Townsend Junior worked as a telegrapher. His job was to send messages along telegraph wires that ran beside the railroad tracks. The telegraph carried the messages in Morse Code, a system of short and long sounds that made up letters, words, and sentences.

From his experience as a telegrapher, John G. Townsend Junior learned that the railroads needed lumber for bridges. He bought forest land in Sussex County

John G. Townsend, Jr.
Courtesy of The Historical Society of Delaware

and went into the lumber business. John Townsend Junior then decided to buy farm land and grow strawberries. He shipped his strawberries on refrigerated railroad cars from Sussex County to big cities like New York and Philadelphia. The refrigerator cars kept the strawberries from spoiling.

Many other Delaware farmers learned to raise new crops that could be taken to market on the railroad. Delaware farmers raised blackberries, peaches, apples, potatoes, and tomatoes. Some of the tomatoes, berries, and fruit went to canneries. Canning became an important industry in southern Delaware. In the canneries, people and machines sorted, washed, and cut up fruit and berries and put them into cans. The cans were shipped on the railroad to city grocery stores. One of Delaware's largest canneries was the Richardson and Robbins Company in Dover. The Richardson and Robbins Cannery is now a state government office building.

A well-known cannery
Courtesy of State of Delaware, Division of Historical and Cultural Affairs

"The Peeling Room," by Howard Pyle
Courtesy of State of Delaware, Division of Historical and Cultural Affairs

Rehoboth Beach,
Courtesy of The Historical Society of Delaware

There is a museum in the building that tells about the history of canning.

People took trips on Delaware's railroads. One of the places that Delawareans most liked to go on the railroad was the seashore. Resort towns grew along Delaware's sea coast. Rehoboth Beach, Dewey Beach, Bethany Beach, and Fenwick Island were all founded during these years.

Around 1900, a family's summer vacation to Rehoboth Beach began with a train ride. The Rehoboth train station was located in the center of town on Rehoboth Avenue about two blocks from the beach. Families could rent rooms in the hotels and houses located near the station. Children enjoyed swimming in the Rehoboth surf just as much then as we do today.

Picnics were also popular summer activities. On the Fourth of July and other summer holidays families went on picnics to beaches along the coast of the Delaware River and Bay. Augustine Beach, Woodland Beach, Bowers Beach, and Kitts Hummock were all popular places for picnics. People who lived in Wilmington traveled to the bay beaches by steamboat. Those who lived on farms or in towns near the bay usually came by

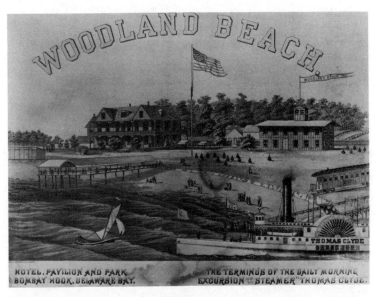

HOTEL, PAVILION AND PARK.
BOMBAY HOOK, DELAWARE BAY.

THE TERMINUS OF THE DAILY MORNING
EXCURSION STEAMER "THOMAS CLYDE."

A Delaware Bay beach resort of the 1890's. What forms of transportation
does the picture show?
Courtesy of Delaware State Archives

horse and buggy. At the picnics adults and children
enjoyed fishing, crabbing, swimming, eating, and playing
games.

Railroads and steamboats were very important to the
city of Wilmington. The biggest industry in Wilmington
was building railroad cars and ships. The companies that
built them were located on the Christina River near the
P. W. & B. railroad tracks. Some of these companies
employed hundreds of workers.

Building a railroad car or a steamboat took teamwork
among people with many different skills. Carpenters,
iron workers, engine builders, upholsterers, and painters
all worked together. The largest of the companies could
build seventy to eighty railroad cars at the same time.
One visitor described the vast size and noise of the
woodworking room at a railroad car factory: "In two
immense rooms, which seem a perfect wilderness of
machinery and ever running, endless belts, wheels are
whirring, and swift steamdriven saws and blades are

A horse and buggy on a street in Dover
Courtesy of The Historical Society of Delaware

eating their way into oaken planks and beams. The shrieking saws and rumbling planers make a wonderful noise.''

After the railroad car or ship was framed out in wood, furniture makers installed seats, beds, lamps, and other finishing touches. Most of the railroad cars built in Wilmington were passenger cars. Some, however, were special cars built for rich people. These special cars were like houses on wheels, complete with beautifully decorated bedrooms, sitting rooms, and dining rooms.

The ships built along the Christina River in Wilmington were also very interesting. Some were steamboats made to carry farm produce to market and passengers on trips to the beach. Others were ferry boats. A few were yachts for rich people. The yachts had beautiful decorations like those in the private railroad cars.

In addition to ships and railroad cars, Wilmington was also famous for tanning hides, making objects from

Building a railroad car in a Wilmington factory
Courtesy of Hagley Museum and Library

iron, and making electric trolley cars. Tanneries made upholstery for seats in railroad cars and ships. The iron workers made railroad car wheels, parts for steam engines, and iron hulls for ships.

By 1900, electric trolley cars were very important in Wilmington and in other American cities. The trolley car was something like a modern bus except that it ran on rails. The trolley car was powered by electricity that ran through an overhead wire. A long pole on the roof of the car, called a "trolley," touched the electrically charged wire and provided power to the motor that moved the car forward.

Before the invention of trolley cars, most people in cities had lived within walking distance of their work. Houses had to be very close together. The trolley cars allowed people to move farther away from where they worked. The new houses built near the trolley lines were spread out and had yards where children could play.

Market Street was the center of Wilmington. All of the trolley car lines started from Market Street and extended like spokes of a wheel to all parts of the city. Market Street was where most of the city's stores,

An electric trolley car on Market Street in downtown Wilmington
Courtesy of Hagley Museum and Library

theaters, restaurants, and hotels were located. When movies were invented, movie theaters were built on Market Street. Wilmington's City Hall was also on Market Street. It was where meetings were held, where the mayor had his office, and where the police and the city jail were located. Today the Old Town Hall is a museum. In the days of the trolley cars, people who lived in and around Wilmington enjoyed coming to Market Street to shop, meet their friends, attend meetings, or go to the movies.

In the summertime the trolley car companies operated amusement parks located just beyond the city at the end of the trolley car lines. There were two amusement parks near Wilmington. They were the Brandywine Springs Park and Shellpot Park. The amusement parks had ponds for boating, places for dances, restaurants, theaters, picnic grounds, and exciting roller coaster rides. People in the city rode the trolley car to get to the parks. On

Old Town Hall in Wilmington, about 1860
Courtesy of The Historical Society of Delaware

holidays such as Memorial Day, the Fourth of July, and Labor Day the amusement parks and the trolley cars were crowded with happy people.

In the years around 1900 many *immigrants* were coming to Wilmington to work in the city's factories. Immigrants are people who move from one country to live in a different country. The immigrants who came to Wilmington in those days came from Europe. Look at a map of Europe and see if you can find the countries from which they came. Many of Wilmington's immigrants came from Ireland. Ireland is an island next to England. Others came from Germany, Poland, Russia, and Italy.

Most of the immigrants from Russia were Jewish. Jewish people began to settle in Wilmington in the 1880s. They built a synagogue in the city and created other Jewish organizations.

The Irish, Poles, and Italians who came to Wilmington were mostly Catholics. They built Catholic churches in the city and named them for the favorite saints from

St. Hedwig's Roman Catholic Church, Wilmington's largest Polish church, looks like many churches in Poland.
Courtesy of The Historical Society of Delaware

their native countries. St. Patrick is the patron saint of Ireland, so Irish immigrants named a church for him. The Polish people named their churches for St. Hedwig and St. Stanislaus, who were important saints in their country. The Italians named their church for St. Anthony of Padua, who was an Italian saint.

Each of the immigrant groups had its own neighborhood in the city. The church or synagogue of each group was built in the center of its neighborhood. Some of these neighborhoods still exist today in Wilmington. St. Anthony of Padua Church is at the center of a

St. Anthony's Roman Catholic Church was built for Wilmington's Italian community. It looks like many churches in Italy.
Courtesy of The Historical Society of Delaware

neighborhood in Wilmington that is called Little Italy. There are many Italian restaurants in that neighborhood. St. Hedwig's Church is at the center of Wilmington's Polish neighborhood. You can find stores that sell Polish food and the headquarters of Polish organizations in that neighborhood.

The immigrants who came to Delaware around 1900 traveled across the ocean from Europe on large steamships. The ships took them to New York City where they saw the Statue of Liberty in the harbor. From New York they came to Wilmington on the train.

Most of the immigrants did not know English so it was hard for them to know where to go in America. Those who came to Wilmington usually had family members living here already. The family members sent the immigrant their address in Wilmington written in English. In New York the immigrant showed the address to the railroad ticket man in order to buy a ticket from New York to Wilmington. When the immigrant got off the train in Wilmington, he or she showed the address to someone in the train station who could point the immigrant in the right direction.

Fortunately the immigrants nearly always found people who could speak their languages and help them find their families or show them how to find a job and a place to stay. Most of the immigrants worked in factories or helped build buildings, roads, or bridges. Some of them laid railroad tracks and trolley car tracks.

By 1900, Wilmington had become an industrial city. It had many houses, factories, stores, and amusements. The city was tied together by the trolley car lines, and Wilmington was linked to other cities and to the rural areas of Delaware by the railroad.

Immigrant getting directions at railroad station

CHAPTER NINETEEN
Big Business Comes to Delaware

THE EARLY YEARS of the twentieth century from 1900 until 1920 saw many changes in Delaware. Automobiles and trucks were beginning to replace the horse and buggy. There were also changes in Delaware's public schools. The one-room schoolhouses were being replaced by larger, more modern school buildings. The way many people worked also began to change. In the past most people had either been farmers or factory workers. During the early twentieth century many people found work in office buildings.

The Du Pont Building in Wilmington was the first large office building in Delaware. The Du Pont Company built this tall, block-long building in 1906. The Du Pont Company was not a new company in 1906. Eleuthère Irénée du Pont had started the company on the Brandywine River over one hundred years earlier in 1802. But the way the company did business was new.

The Du Pont Building, 1920
Courtesy of Hagley Museum and Library

T. Coleman du Pont in an automobile
Courtesy of Hagley Museum and Library

Do you remember reading about the lives of Du Pont workers at Hagley? In those days the workers lived close to the mills. The power that ran the mills came from the water in the Brandywine River. Eleuthère Irénée du Pont ran the whole powderyard business from a small one-room office building.

By 1906 all this had changed. Waterpower had been replaced by steam power and electric power. Steam and electricity could produce far more power than the Brandywine River could produce. The company's new factories were much larger. Machinery did more of the work and workmen did less. The Du Pont Company's factories were located all over the United States. They were bound together by telephone, telegraph, and railroad.

The big office building in Wilmington was the center for the company's many factories. The people who worked in the office building included accountants who kept track of the company's bills and receipts. Others were managers who decided where to build new factories, what products to make, and how to get people to buy those products. Most of the office workers lived too far from the Du Pont Building to walk to work. They came to work on the trolley car or in automobiles.

The Du Pont Company had become a big business. There were many other big businesses in the United States by the early twentieth century. The Du Pont Company was the biggest business in Delaware. In the years from 1914-1918, there was a war in Europe that we call the First World War or World War I. As the largest American maker of gunpowder, the Du Pont Company made a great deal of money during World War I. The company also hired more workers and built more factories.

The presidents of the Du Pont Company during these years were T. Coleman du Pont and Pierre S. du Pont. These men became very wealthy. They used the money they earned to make Delaware a more modern state.

Pierre S. du Pont
Courtesy of The Historical Society of Delaware

In the early twentieth century, gasoline-powered automobiles were a new invention. In those days only a few rich people could afford to own an automobile. T. Coleman du Pont loved automobiles. He believed that one day many people would own them. He knew that Delaware would need paved roads before that day came. He also believed that trucks would be as important to the farmers of the twentieth century as the railroad and steamboats had been to Delaware's farmers in the century before.

In 1911, T. Coleman du Pont told the Delaware General Assembly that he wanted to build a modern highway for Delaware. The Assembly could hardly believe that anyone would give the state a free highway. But that is what T. Coleman du Pont did. The highway he built is called the Du Pont Highway, which today is Route 13 from Claymont in the north to Dover, and Route 113 south of Dover to Selbyville. Construction crews began building the highway in southern Sussex County. They laid the concrete road through swamps, forests, and farmland. The highway was completed to Wilmington in 1924.

Building the Du Pont Highway

Mrs. Cecile A. Steele, her children, and caretaker Ike Long, with her
broiler chickens
Courtesy of The University of Delaware

The Du Pont Highway was Delaware's first modern
paved road. After it was built the state of Delaware built
many other paved roads that connected with the Du Pont
Highway.

Just as T. Coleman du Pont had hoped, the Du Pont
Highway was very important to farmers. The highway
encouraged the use of trucks that could take crops from
the farm to the city quickly.

Because of this rapid transportation, farmers in Sussex County began raising *broiler chickens* in the 1920s.
Today broilers are the most important farm crop in
Delaware. The first person to raise broiler chickens was
Mrs. Cecile Steele of Ocean View. Broiler chickens
are very young chickens that weigh no more than three
pounds. Since the chickens eat corn and soybeans, Delaware's farmers grow these crops. Factories in southern
Delaware and nearby Maryland kill the chickens, remove their feathers, and prepare them for market. Big
trucks carry the chickens up the Du Pont Highway to
Philadelphia, New York, and Boston.

Pierre S. du Pont High School
Courtesy of The Historical Society of Delaware

T. Coleman du Pont's highway is very important for Delaware. T. Coleman du Pont once said, "I'm going to build a monument a hundred miles high and lay it down on the ground." He did just that.

T. Coleman du Pont's cousin, Pierre S. du Pont, was also interested in helping Delaware. He believed that the one-room schoolhouse was old fashioned, just like the horse and buggy. P. S. du Pont decided to build new and bigger schools for the towns of Delaware. He paid for many new schools in the state. You may be a student in one of Pierre S. du Pont's schools. If not, one of his schools is probably still standing and in use near where you live. The schools that Pierre S. du Pont built were usually brick buildings with many windows in every room. Each school contained an auditorium, a gymnasium, a cafeteria, and other special rooms. Can you imagine how strange and exciting it must have been for children to go to such a school after attending a one-room school!?

In 1914 there was another big improvement in education in Delaware: the opening of the Women's College in Newark. The Women's College is now part of the University of Delaware. It offered young women in Delaware the chance to get a college education. Many

A building of The Woman's College of The University of Delaware built in
1914
Courtesy of The Historical Society of Delaware

of the teachers who taught in the new schools studied at
the Women's College.

In addition to building schools in Delaware, Pierre S.
du Pont also created beautiful gardens at his home at
Longwood Gardens. Longwood Gardens is near Kennett
Square, Pennsylvania, just over the Delaware border.

Cars on Market Street in the 1920's
Courtesy of Hagley Museum and Library

There are many kinds of gardens and flowers at Longwood. It is an interesting place to visit if you like plants and flowers.

By the 1920s, Delaware was very different from Delaware in 1900. Office buildings, paved streets, automobiles, trucks, and large new school buildings changed the state. People could not do office work unless they could read, write, and do arithmetic. The better schools prepared Delaware's children for the new office jobs. Since offices were located in cities and towns, more people moved to the city.

Life on the farm changed, too. The new highways helped farmers to make more money from their crops. With the money they bought cars, trucks, and tractors. They sent their children to the new schools, where they learned how science could improve farming. All of Delaware was becoming modern. The horse and buggy days were a thing of the past.

CHAPTER TWENTY

Delaware during and after World War II

D URING THE 1930s, a dictator named Adolf Hitler became the ruler of Germany. Hitler created a large German army. His army attacked nearly all the countries in Europe. The German army conquered many countries. Two countries in Europe, England and Russia, fought back so that Hitler could not conquer either one.

Germany's ally was Japan. *Allies* are countries that form a partnership to protect themselves from other countries. Japan is an island nation in the Pacific Ocean near Asia. See if you can find Japan on a map. Japan tried to conquer China and other countries in Asia. The German and Japanese attacks on their neighbors brought on World War II, which lasted from September 1939 until August 1945.

For the first two years of World War II, the United States did not take sides because the war was not in America. Then, on December 7, 1941, Japanese airplanes bombed American ships at Pearl Harbor in the Hawaiian Islands. Americans were shocked by this attack and declared war. The United States became an ally of England, Russia, and China against Japan and Germany.

World War II was the biggest war in history. Winning the war took the effort of everyone in America. Delaware played an important role in winning World War II.

During World War II, 30,000 Delawareans served in the armed forces—the U. S. Army, Army Air Force, Navy, and Marines. Delawareans fought in all the campaigns of the war. Two Delaware sailors were killed in the Japanese attack at Pearl Harbor. Another Delawar-

The Japanese attack at Pearl Harbor, December 7, 1941
Courtesy of the National Archives

ean, an army airplane pilot, shot down four of the attacking Japanese planes at Pearl Harbor.

Shortly after the attack on Pearl Harbor, a regiment of Delaware soldiers was sent to the island of Bora Bora in the Pacific Ocean. This regiment, the 198th Coast Artillery, fought against the Japanese through the war. Their main job was to fire artillery guns at Japanese airplanes. Soldiers and sailors from Delaware fought in other parts of the world also. Delawareans fought in the American army that pushed the Germans out of North Africa in 1943. They also fought against the Germans in Europe.

During World War II, the Germans sent submarines into the Atlantic Ocean to sink the ships of America and her allies. The German submarines, or U-boats as the Germans called them, sank many allied ships carrying supplies and soldiers to Europe. Some U-boats came very close to the coast of Delaware.

To battle the U-boats, the United States Army built Fort Miles on the sand dunes of Cape Henlopen near Lewes. The Army built a series of towers along Delaware's seashore. The towers were used to sight U-boats so that the big guns at Fort Miles could fire on them. At night soldiers patrolled the beach at Rehoboth to keep

Delaware troops on Bora Bora in the Pacific Ocean, 1942-43
Courtesy of Delaware State Archives

Fort Miles towers on Delaware beach
Courtesy of Delaware State Archives

the Germans from landing. Fortunately, the Germans did not land. But they did damage American shipping. Eventually most of the U-boats were sunk by the United States Navy. One, however, surrendered at Fort Miles when the war ended in 1945.

In addition to Fort Miles, there were several Army Air Force bases in Delaware. The New Castle County Army Air Base is now the Greater Wilmington Airport. During World War II the air base was used to ferry planes and supplies from the United States to Europe. Among the Army pilots who flew from the New Castle County Air Base was a group of women. They were the WASPs, which stands for Women's Air Force Service Pilots.

Just below Dover in Kent County, the Army built the Dover Airfield. This airfield is now the huge Dover Air Force Base. The Dover Airfield was a training field for pilots. It was also used for the secret testing of America's first rockets.

Delaware also took part in the war by making supplies for the Army and Navy. Wilmington's shipyards were kept very busy. Many of the landing craft that brought soldiers and marines to enemy beaches were built on the Christina River in Wilmington.

Wilmington was also the home of America's three largest explosives makers, the Du Pont Company, Atlas Powder Company, and the Hercules Powder Company. These companies supplied most of the ammunition used by the United States Army and Navy.

Delaware companies helped the war effort in other ways as well. The Du Pont Company, for example, made nylon, which was the material used in parachutes. A chemist at the Du Pont Company invented nylon just before the war started. The company built its first nylon plant in Seaford, Delaware, in 1939. The Du Pont Company also built the plant in Washington state where the first atomic bomb was made.

WASPs at New Castle Army Air Base, 1944-45
Courtesy of Delaware State Archives

By dropping two atomic bombs on Japan, the United States forced Japan to surrender in August 1945. Germany had already surrendered in April 1945. World War II was over. The soldiers and sailors were released from the armed services. American companies stopped making materials for war and went back to making things like automobiles, refrigerators, and houses.

The years just after World War II are called the *postwar years*. The postwar years were an important time in the history of Delaware and of the whole United States. During the postwar years there were many new jobs in Delaware and people from all over the United States moved here.

In the postwar years many more people owned automobiles than ever before. Two automobile assembly plants were built in New Castle County, a General Motors plant near Wilmington, and a Chrysler plant in Newark.

The Chrysler Corporation's Newark Assembly Plant
Courtesy of The Chrysler Corporation

On the assembly line at General Motors
Courtesy of the Delaware Development Office

People who owned cars could live in places that had no trolley car or bus transportation. Suburbs were built beyond Delaware's towns and cities where farms had once been. Many suburban housing developments were built around Wilmington in New Castle County. Most people who lived in the suburbs went to work in their automobiles. People also used their automobiles to go shopping, to go to the movies, and to go to the beach.

With so many cars, parking became a problem in cities and towns. One way to solve the parking problem was to move stores, theaters, factories, and office buildings out of the city into the suburbs. Shopping centers, shopping malls, and industrial parks were built in Delaware, especially around Wilmington.

The new shopping centers had big parking lots that made them convenient to use. People went to the shopping centers and malls and stopped shopping in towns and cities. Main streets in every town in Delaware lost business. Market Street in Wilmington, once the center of shopping in Delaware, lost its customers. One by one the movie theaters on Market Street closed down. Many stores on Market Street were boarded up.

Automobiles and suburbs could not exist without highways. In the postwar years Delaware built many new highways and expanded old ones. One of the most spectacular new roadways for cars was not a highway at all, but the Delaware Memorial Bridge, which opened in 1951.

The Delaware Memorial Bridge is a memorial to the soldiers and sailors from Delaware who died fighting in World War II. It spans the Delaware River, connecting Delaware to New Jersey. The bridge replaced a ferry service that once carried cars and trucks across the river. It was fun to ride on the ferry boat, but it was slow.

By the 1960s, traffic on the Delaware Memorial Bridge was so great that Delaware had to build a second bridge next to the first one. Together these bridges are called the Delaware Memorial Bridges. In the 1980s, well over 20 million cars and trucks crossed the twin bridges every year. For many travelers passing through Delaware, the Delaware Memorial Bridges are a memorable sight.

Another important highway project in Delaware was the construction of the interstate highway, I-95. This highway is part of a national system of high-speed interstate highways that was built between the 1950s and the 1970s. I-95 connects Delaware with all three of its neighboring states, Maryland, Pennsylvania, and New Jersey.

Delaware Memorial Bridge, 1951
Courtesy of The Historical Society of Delaware

I-95 passing through Brandywine Hundred, 1968
Courtesy of Temple University Press

Legislative Hall, Dover, Delaware. The State Senate and House of
Representatives meet in this building. The Governor's office is there also.
Courtesy of Delaware State Archives

Inside Legislative Hall, The House of Representatives in session.
Courtesy of Delaware Development Office

UNIT SEVEN

DELAWARE TODAY

CHAPTER TWENTY-ONE
Delaware's State Government

YOU NOW KNOW a lot about the history of Delaware. In this unit you will learn about Delaware today. You will learn how our state government works. You will also learn about Delaware's role in the government of our country, the United States of America.

State government in Delaware is divided into three parts. They are the General Assembly, the Governor and his or her officers, and the judges.

The General Assembly is the legislature of Delaware. It makes Delaware's laws. There are two houses in the General Assembly. They are the Senate and the House of Representatives. There are 21 Senators and 41 Representatives. People are elected to the General Assembly from districts in all parts of the state. Members of the House of Representatives serve two year terms. Members of the Senate serve four year terms. The leader of the Senate is the lieutenant-governor. The leader of the House of Representatives is called the Speaker of the House.

The General Assembly meets in Legislative Hall in Dover. The Senate meets in a room on one side of the building, and the House of Representatives meets in a room on the other side of the building. There is a balcony above each room where anyone, including you, can go to watch the meetings.

Lieutenant Governor S.B. Woo
Courtesy of the Office of the Lieutenant Governor, State of Delaware

Governor Michael N. Castle visits a school
Courtesy of the Office of the Governor, State of Delaware

The General Assembly meets every year from January through June. The General Assembly makes many important decisions. It makes laws about crimes. It decides how to raise money to run the state government. The General Assembly also decides how much money to give to each part of the government.

After the General Assembly passes a bill, it sends it to the governor. If the governor signs the bill, it becomes the law. If the governor does not like the bill, he or she does not sign it. This is called a *veto*. If the General Assembly passes the bill again by a vote of two thirds or more, they can override the governor's veto and the bill becomes law.

The second part of Delaware's government is the governor and the governor's cabinet officers. The governor has the most important job in Delaware. The governor is elected for a four year term. The governor is in charge of carrying out the laws that the General Assembly makes. The governor also appoints the judges and other important officials and is in charge of important ceremonies in our state.

The governor works with a group of officers who help to run the state. One of these officers is the attorney general. The attorney general's job is to make sure that the laws are obeyed. Delaware's state police force helps to enforce the laws. You have probably seen state policemen in their blue uniforms directing traffic on the highways. Another officer of the state is in charge of health and welfare. The state runs a hospital at Farnhurst and the Delaware Hospital for the Chronically Ill at Smyrna. There are other agencies as well that help sick people and old people.

Two of the most important activities of state government are building and maintaining highways and providing public education. The Department of Transportation is in charge of highways. Sometimes the department's name is shortened to Del. D.O.T. Look for the words

The Delaware State Police
Courtesy of E.A. Vassas, Delaware State Police

Del. D.O.T. on signs where roads are being built or widened.

The State Board of Education is in charge of public education in Delaware. The State Board of Education makes the rules for the public schools. The state is divided into a number of school districts. Each district is allowed to make some rules itself. Each school district is run by a superintendent and a board of education elected by the people of the district. The board makes rules and the superintendent sees that they are followed.

The third part of the state government is made up of the courts and judges. There are several different courts in Delaware. The most important court is the State Supreme Court. Other important courts are the Superior Court and the Court of Chancery. The judges who run these courts are appointed by the governor. In some courts a jury of twelve citizens may decide the winner of the case. Other times the judge decides the case.

Each county has a county seat where the state courts meet. In New Castle County, the courts meet in Wil-

Inside the Old Court House in New Castle
The News-Journal Company

mington. In Kent County, they meet in Dover, and in Sussex County, they meet in Georgetown.

Now you know about the three parts of the state government. But the most important thing to know about the government is that it is responsible to the people. The governor, the lieutenant-governor, the attorney general, and the members of the General Assembly are all elected by the people. Long ago women and black men could not vote. But now every citizen over 18 years of age can vote and take part in the government.

Most of the people who run for public office belong to a political party. There are two major political parties in Delaware. They are the Republican Party and the Democratic Party. Each party nominates a candidate for all the elected jobs in the government. For example, the Republicans choose a candidate for governor and the Democrats also choose a candidate. The voters decide which candidate they want to hold the office.

Elections are held in Delaware on the first Tuesday in November. Two days after the election for president and

Return Day in Georgetown Delaware
Courtesy of Delaware Development Office

governor, Delaware holds a big celebration called *Return Day*. Return Day is held in the Courthouse Circle in Georgetown in Sussex County. Delaware is the only state that has a Return Day celebration.

The name Return Day means that it is the day when all the returns, or votes, from the election are counted and announced. A man in old-fashioned clothes and a silk hat announces the winners of the state elections from the courthouse steps. The winning and losing candidates ride together in a parade into town in horse-drawn carriages past cheering people. Everybody has a good time eating roast beef, oysters, and other food. The winners probably have an even better time than the losers.

CHAPTER TWENTY-TWO
Delaware in the Nation

DELAWARE WAS THE first state to accept the Constitution of the United States. That makes Delaware the First State. Now there are fifty states in the United States of America. You might say that forty-nine other states have joined little Delaware to form a big, powerful country.

The government of the United States is often called the *federal* government. Federal government means the government of all the states combined.

The United States federal government is organized into three parts just like Delaware's state government. The United States government is located in Washington, D. C. The leader of the United States federal government is the President of the United States. The president's job is something like that of a state governor only much bigger because he works for all the states.

The legislature of the United States is called Congress. Congress is divided into two houses, the United States House of Representatives and the United States

The United States Capitol in Washington, D.C.
Courtesy of the National Graphic Center and The Office of U.S. Senator William V. Roth, Jr.

U.S. District Court Judge Jane R. Roth
Courtesy of the Office of U.S. District Court, Judge Jane R. Roth

Senate. The division is just like the division of the state General Assembly into its two houses.

The federal government also has its own courts and judges. There are United States District Courts in every state in the Union. The United States District Court for Delaware is located in Wilmington. Cases that are not resolved in the District Court go to the United States Court of Appeals. The hardest cases go to the United States Supreme Court in Washington, D.C. The United States Supreme Court has final authority to resolve federal cases.

Delaware takes part in all three parts of the federal government. Delaware's voters elect one representative to the United States House of Representatives. Representatives are elected for a two-year term of office. Delaware voters also elect two United States Senators. Senators serve a six-year term of office.

Delaware's voters also help to elect the President of the United States. No one from Delaware has ever been elected president. Perhaps someday a Delawarean will be chosen to sit in the White House. The *White House* is the building in Washington, D. C., where the president lives and where the president's office is located.

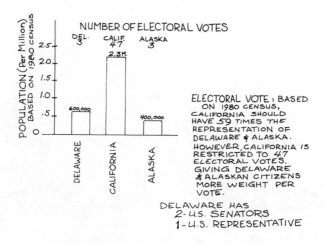

POPULATION (Per Million) BASED ON 1980 CENSUS

NUMBER OF ELECTORAL VOTES

DEL. 3   CALIF. 47   ALASKA 3

2.3 M.

600,000   400,000

ELECTORAL VOTE: BASED ON 1980 CENSUS, CALIFORNIA SHOULD HAVE 59 TIMES THE REPRESENTATION OF DELAWARE & ALASKA. HOWEVER, CALIFORNIA IS RESTRICTED TO 47 ELECTORAL VOTES, GIVING DELAWARE & ALASKAN CITIZENS MORE WEIGHT PER VOTE.

DELAWARE HAS
2-U.S. SENATORS
1-U.S. REPRESENTATIVE

DELAWARE   CALIFORNIA   ALASKA

Chart showing Delaware's Representative and Senators and electoral votes

The federal government is not just located in Washington, D.C. There are branches of the federal government in every state, even in every town. Do you have a United States Post Office in your town or city? The post office is a part of the federal government.

The federal government is involved in the State of Delaware in many ways. Federal programs help poor people and provide some of the money for public schools. The federal government supplied most of the money to build the interstate highway, I-95, through Delaware. The Dover Air Force Base is run by the federal government. The Dover Air Force Base is the home of the largest airplanes in the American Air Force. These planes carry huge amounts of cargo to Europe and other distant places.

People in the United States sometimes disagree about what things they would like the federal government to do and what things they want the state government to do. The jobs of the federal government and the state government are often related. The two governments work together to solve problems. The partnership between the federal government and the state government has helped to make Delaware what it is today.

The White House, Washington, D.C.
Courtesy of the Office of U.S. Senator William V. Roth, Jr.

The Federal Building in Wilmington
Courtesy of Delaware Development Office

CHAPTER TWENTY-THREE

Keeping Delaware's Heritage

IN THE BEGINNING of this book you learned about the geography of Delaware. You learned how important the Delaware Bay and Delaware River were to the Indians and to the early European settlers. You also learned about the fields, forests, and marshlands that once covered Delaware. In this chapter you will learn how water, marshlands, fields, and forests are still important to Delaware's people today.

Just west of the Indian River Bay in Sussex County is the home of the Nanticoke Indians. Today many Nan-

Modern Nanticoke Indians at Powwow
Courtesy of Delaware Development Office

197

ticoke Indian families own farms that raise corn, soybeans, tomatoes, chickens, and other crops. Some of
these crops are the same crops that their ancestors grew
a long time ago. But now the Indians use modern tractors to plant their seeds and harvest their crops. They do
not live in wigwams but in modern houses. Some
Nanticoke Indians are schoolteachers, truck drivers, and
gas station owners.

The Nanticoke Indians have modernized their way of
life, but they have not forgotten how the Indians lived
long ago. They still meet together as a tribe. The
Nanticokes still hold ceremonies or powwows where
they dress in Indian clothing and paint their faces and
bodies just as their ancestors did in the past. The
Nanticoke Indians keep their old ways because their
traditions help them to keep their community together

Dr. Jonathan Pennock, aboard the *Cape Henlopen*, collects a water sample
from Delaware Bay. His work will help the University of Delaware's
College of Marine Studies gain a better understanding of the health of
the bay.
Courtesy of Bob Bowden, Pollution Ecology Laboratory, College of Marine
Studies, University of Delaware, Lewes

Trussum Pond in Sussex County
Courtesy of The Historical Society of Delaware

and tell them who they are and where they come from.

Not everybody in Delaware has a past culture as exciting as that of the Nanticoke Indians. But all of us have a history that is important to who we are today. This is true no matter who your ancestors were. They all had a part in making the world we know now.

Do you remember how we learned that the Indians had great respect for nature? Today, it is very important that all Delawareans respect nature. The future of our state depends on it.

Today, there are many more people in Delaware than there were long ago. There are ten times more people in Delaware now than there were at the time of the Revolutionary War. There are many big cities close to our state. New York, Philadelphia, Baltimore, and Washington, D. C., are all near Delaware. These cities have many people and industries.

Delawareans are being very careful to make sure that nature is not damaged by people and factories. It is

Bombay Hook Wildlife Refuge
Courtesy of Delaware Development Office

especially important to protect the area along Delaware's coast.

In 1971, the General Assembly passed an important law called the Coastal Zone Act. The law keeps wetland marshes along the coast of the Delaware Bay and Delaware River free from factories. Thanks to the Coastal Zone Act, the fish and birds will continue to live in the wetlands. Many of the fish that are born in the wetlands swim out to the ocean and are important to the whole Atlantic Ocean.

The University of Delaware has a laboratory in Lewes, Delaware, where scientists study ways to help the fish, crabs, oysters, and other water creatures live. This work is very important to keeping the oceans healthy. It is also important for the fishermen who catch fish, crabs, and oysters so that you can eat them.

The State of Delaware and the federal government have created a number of parks to take care of our forests, marshes, and wildlife. One of these parks is the Bombay Hook National Wildlife Refuge, which covers a large wetland area along the Delaware Bay in Kent County. If you visit Bombay Hook you will see many different kinds of birds. Some birds live there year-round. Others stop at the refuge as they migrate south in the fall and north in the spring. You will see many ducks and geese swimming on the ponds at Bombay Hook. You may also see bald eagles there. The bald eagle is the national symbol of the United States. There are not many bald eagles living in our country anymore. It is important to give them a safe place to live. Bombay Hook is a safe place for birds.

There are also state parks in Delaware. At Trap Pond State Park in Sussex County you can paddle a canoe past cypress trees growing in swamp waters. At Sussex County's Seashore State Park you can walk along the sand dunes on the beach and swim in the ocean. In New Castle County's Brandywine State Park you can walk on paths along the Brandywine River and through forests and fields like those of long ago.

The people of Delaware want to keep our state beautiful. We want to keep our forests, beaches, marshes, and wildlife. Just like the Indians of long ago, we need the clean water that comes from our rivers and from under the ground. This is the water we drink, cook with, and wash in. We need the fish and other wildlife for food. We need to have farms that produce crops to feed the many people in our state and in the nearby big cities.

Today Delaware has many industries. We have automobile factories, chemical factories, and food processing factories. We also have banks and other businesses.

Delaware's factories and businesses continue to bring new people to our state from other parts of the United States and from other countries. Today there are Delawareans who came from Puerto Rico, an American island in the Caribbean sea. Look for Puerto Rico on a map of North and South America. People in Puerto Rico speak Spanish. Many of the Puerto Ricans who have come to Delaware live in Wilmington.

Another important group of newcomers to Delaware is people from Asia, especially from China, Taiwan, and Korea. In 1984, Dr. S. B. Woo, a Delawarean born

Texaco's Delaware City refinery
Courtesy of Texaco USA

in China, was elected the lieutenant-governor of Delaware. Dr. Woo is a scientist who teaches at the University of Delaware.

Delawareans today are very proud of their state. In spite of its small size, Delaware has a great deal of variety. Delaware has ocean beaches in the south and rolling hills in the north. Our state has many kinds of businesses and factories. Delaware's farms grow many kinds of crops. The state's people are varied, too. There are Delawareans whose ancestors were native American Indians. Other Delawareans had ancestors who came to our state from the continents of Africa, Europe, and Asia.

International Hispanic food festival
Courtesy of Parish of St. Paul, Wilmington

On the boardwalk at Rehoboth Beach
Courtesy of Delaware Development Office

We cannot see into Delaware's future. It will be up to you and your classmates to make the future of our state. It is important for you to know about Delaware's past and present so that you can make its future a good one.

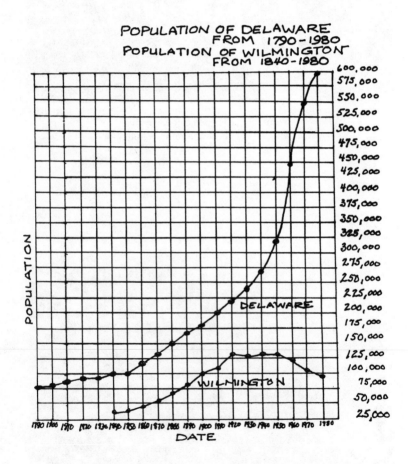

Chart showing population of Delaware

THE AMERICAN HOLLY, DELAWARE'S STATE TREE

The American holly is an evergreen tree that grows in Delaware's forests. The holly tree's red berries and sharp-pointed green leaves are very beautiful and make the tree easy to recognize. Holly trees grow in all three of Delaware's counties but are most often found in southern Delaware. Holly trees like southern Delaware's sandy soil and ocean breezes. They grow in forests under tall pine trees. Cuttings from holly trees make very good decorations at Christmas-time.

Courtesy of the Delaware State Archives

THE BLUE HEN'S CHICKEN, DELAWARE'S STATE BIRD

Between battles and marches, soldiers in the Revolutionary War entertained themselves with cock fights. In a cock fight, two roosters are put in a pit to fight one another. Soldiers from the different states carried their best fighting roosters with them.

The soldiers from Delaware carried roosters of a breed called blue hens. The blue hens had blue-colored feathers. They were tough, brave birds that seldom lost a fight. The soldiers from Delaware wore blue coats and were brave fighters. They reminded people of their fighting blue hens. The Delaware soldiers were proud to be called the "Blue Hens' Chickens."

Since the Revolutionary War the Blue Hen's chicken has become the symbol of Delaware. That is why the sports teams of the University of Delaware are known as the "Fighting Blue Hens."

Courtesy of the Delaware State Archives

THE DELAWARE
STATE FLAG

The Delaware state flag shows many symbols of our state and its history. The state flag has two major colors, blue and buff. These were the colors of the Delaware soldiers' uniforms in the Revolutionary War. In the center of the flag is the state's coat of arms in a diamond. The diamond shape is used because Delaware is called the Diamond State. The diamond, like Delaware, is small but valuable. Below the diamond it says: "December 7, 1787." This is the date when Delaware became the first state to ratify the United States Constitution.

The state seal shows two men on either side of a shield. The man on the right is a militia man. He holds a rifle. The man on the left is a farmer. He holds a hoe. The two men represent what people did in Delaware before the Revolutionary War. Above the shield is a ship and three sacks of flour. Inside the shield you will see an ear of corn, a sheaf of wheat, and an ox. These things all represent Delaware's crops and trade. Below the shield is the Delaware state motto, "Liberty and Independence." This motto appeared on the hats worn by Delaware's soldiers in the Revolutionary War.

Courtesy of the Delaware State Archives

THE PEACH BLOSSOM, DELAWARE'S STATE FLOWER

During the 1800s Delaware farmers planted peach orchards all through the state. Peaches were harvested in the summer and shipped on steamboats and the railroads to big city markets in Baltimore, Philadelphia, and New York. Some farmers became wealthy growing this delicious fruit. In the 1870s, a disease called "the yellows" destroyed many of the state's peach trees.

The beautiful, sweet-smelling peach blossom is Delaware's state flower. Today, Delaware's farmers are again growing peaches, although not as many as in the past. The fresh peaches you buy at a market stand might have come from a Delaware peach tree.

Courtesy of the Delaware State Archives

THE LADYBUG, DELAWARE'S STATE INSECT

The ladybug is a small beetle that has a round body. The ladybug's body is very colorful. It is covered with spots. Most of Delaware's ladybugs have red bodies and black spots. Ladybugs are helpful to fruit growers because they eat the lice that feed on the leaves of fruit trees. A class of Delaware school children asked the state legislature to make the ladybug Delaware's state insect.

Index

LIBERTY AND INDEPENDENCE